DICT

FOODS

by

BENGAMIN GAYELORD HAUSER
and
RAGNAR BERG

Benedict Lust Publications, New York, N.Y. 10016

DICTIONARY OF FOODS
Paperback Edition © Copyright 1970
BY BENEDICT LUST PUBLICATIONS
Library of Congress Catalog Number 75-131930

A BENEFICIAL BOOK Edition
First printing...............July 1970

This Beneficial Book edition includes all the text and tables
of the original higher-priced hard cover edition.
It is printed from brand new plates in clear, easy-to-read type.
Beneficial Books are published in pocket book form by a division
of Benedict Lust Publications, Box 404, New York, N.Y. 10016

Printed in the United States of America

CONTENTS

PROUDLY WE PRESENT

VERY frequently a movement for human betterment appears and fades out with dismaying suddenness for want of a leader.

Frequently, too, such a movement is given tremendous impetus because of the leadership of some brave and brilliant mind and then dies down like the machinery of a child's toy when that personality disappears and the strong hand which guided its course is relaxed from the controls.

The movement for a sane, natural approach to health is fortunate in three respects: It has a leader. It has an articulate leader. It has a leader whose influence will survive even the ravages of time.

For many years Bengamin Gayelord Hauser, a brilliant Viennese food scientist and internationally famous health authority, has been lecturing to thousands of people on both sides of the Atlantic. The celebrated Hauser method of Eliminative Feeding for health and power, the theory of Harmonized Food Selections, the revolutionary discoveries of the influence of food on types and temperaments—all these have established Bengamin Gayelord Hauser as a leader. His easily balanced erudition and personal magnetism, which breeds respect and commands attention, have made him one of the most effective health teachers of the day.

He has the rare ability to project this personality into the cold medium of a scientific book; he has the happy faculty of making science fascinating enough to be avidly read and understandable enough to be used in everyday life. He thus offers in a permanent form the main tenets of his philosophy. He builds a strong foundation on which a new understanding of health can be superimposed in future years.

The cornerstone of this broad foundation is a monumental work which Hauser has recently completed in collaboration with Ragnar Berg— his DICTIONARY OF FOODS.

No set of theories can earn the standing of a science unless it possess a standard work, a definite explanation of terms and new, original information by which the theories can be backed. THE DICTIONARY OF FOODS does just that for the science of modern living.

JOHN B. LUST,
Editor & Publisher

FOREWORD

HIPPOCRATES, the father of medicine, may also be justly called the father of food science; for it was he who first said, "Your food shall be your medicine." Twenty years ago this statement was paraphrased by that great man, Dr. Wiley, of the Bureau of Chemistry in Washington, when he declared, "Foods will be the medicine of the future."

It was Hippocrates who first used different foods for the healing of the sick. The practical knowledge of foods which he gave the world was more or less followed until the middle of the last century when a new interest, I might say renaissance, in scientific food research began.

Dating from this renaissance, food science, as we know it today, is comparatively young. The first constructive work in this field was done in 1840 by Justus von Liebig who made his first food analysis in his laboratory in Giessen, Germany. Next, Carl von Voit improved upon Liebig's work, but it remained for the great physiologist, Rubner, to enlarge, and to some extent perfect, the researches of his two predecessors.

Up to this time, however, it was believed that an adult needed 180 grams of protein, 56 grams of fat and 500 grams of carbohydrates to supply his daily needs. This teaching was most unfortunate, especially since meat was then thought to be the best source of protein (a false belief which still remains in the mass mind even today). At about the same time, too, denatured foods such as white bread, erroneously supposed to have great food values, were introduced and quickly gained popular favor. As a result, many previously unknown diseases, such as gout and diabetes, increased by leaps and bounds.

To counteract this meat-eating craze to which Europe, and later on practically the whole world, had succumbed, vegetarianism came into vogue. Because vegetarianism has always been the subject of so much controversy and has given rise to so many conflicting ideas and also because it has been more or less associated with cults, the great mass of people have not as yet become interested in it. It was such pioneers as Bircher Benner of Zurich, H. Lahmann of Dresden and later D. J. Kellog here in America who identified themselves with vegetarianism and gave it its modern standing as a science.

The next to whom the world owes a great debt for their important discoveries are R. H. Chittenden and I. Fischer of America and M. Hindhede of Denmark. The credit for the revolutionary discovery of vitamins belongs to Casimir Funk of London and E. V. McCollum of Baltimore. Last, but by no means least, is that great scientist, Dr. Ragnar Berg, who through his original food analyses has been able to find out whether or not a food had an alkali or acid excess and to discover the presence and proportions of food mineral elements.

This Dictionary of Foods is the first of its kind. It has been prepared with the personal help and collaboration of Dr. Berg. Its purpose is to inform the layman just what chemicals predominate in the foods we eat; and whenever possible, to give the special curative value in those foods that can be used in overcoming specific conditions.

People, living in all parts of the country, are writing to me asking for the analyses of different foods. This dictionary combined with the chemical chart will answer all your questions. No space is taken up by needless theory, as theories only tend to bewilder the reader. I have even refrained from giving the caloric standard, as I find it of little value in practical, applied food science.

Now, a few words in regard to Dr. Berg, the co-author of this book. Because of his original and fearless ideas, this great scientist has received the recognition of the world. The City of Dresden has established a laboratory for him in order that he may continue his valuable researches into the mysteries of the chemical make-up of foods. In this laboratory much constructive work is being done. The newest analyses of foods are the result of his many years of painstaking work.

I hope that my American students will appreciate the tremendous and detailed amount of laboratory research and experimentation involved in the preparation of this Dictionary of Foods; and it is fitting here that I express my heartfelt thanks to Dr. Ragnar Berg, the co-author, for the personal help and valuable information which he has so freely given me.

BENGAMIN GAYELORD HAUSER.

DICTIONARY OF FOODS

ACORN

Nut of various oak trees of the *quercus* species; rich in incomplete protein and fat; very rich in phosphorus and sulphur; having high acid excess and small percentages of vitamins A and B. Since acorns are very rich in tannic acid they have an astringent or "binding" effect upon the bowels. For this reason they have been used as a popular remedy for diarrhea. Because they tend to bring on constipation they are not a popular food, and are only consumed when the crops in poverty-stricken countries fail.

Acorns should be boiled or rinsed and then washed in lye in order to free them from the bitter tannin before eating. Some acorns, especially certain varieties found in Southern Spain and North America, have a pleasant, sweet taste.

Owing to their astringent or "binding" properties acorns are used as an addition to health cocoa and chocolate. When thoroughly roasted and ground they also serve as a substitute for coffee. For no logical reason "acorn coffee" has been recommended as curative measure for those suffering from tuberculosis of the lungs (consumption), trembling, rickets, bone weakness, anemia and nervous conditions. It is, however, helpful in overcoming certain intestinal disorders such as chronic diarrhea.

AGAR-AGAR

A species of sea grass, often called Japanese gelatin or vegetable gelatin. It consists mainly of carbohydrates, called gelose, and for cooking purposes must first be dissolved in hot water. It is derived from the Japanese and Indian species of sea algae, and contains traces of iodine. In the fresh state many of these algae are eaten by the Japanese. Dried agar-agar swells to many times its size when it reaches the intestines, and for that reason is often used as a bulk food for the relief of constipation. Powdered agar-agar should be used in the place of the questionable animal gelatins.

ALE

Fermented extracts obtained from germinated, starchy seeds; an infusion of malt (grain, generally barley) usually with the addition of hops; a stimulating alcoholic beverage; containing an excessive amount of phosphorus acid and a very slight trace of vitamin B.

Ale has no special health-giving properties. In fact, if it is consumed regularly over a long period of time, it is positively harmful to the body.

ALMOND

Kernel of the ripe nuts of the *prunus nana* and its varieties; containing a large percentage of protein, much fat and only small quantities of vitamins A and B; having an acid excess. Almonds can be eaten to supply the necessary protein to those who follow a strictly vegetarian diet, but due to the fact that they are so rich in protein and have an excessive acid content they should be eaten sparingly by non-vegetarians. Twenty grams of almonds have approximately the same nutritive value as one egg. Since they are very difficult to digest they must be well chewed. Almonds should be finely ground before they are given to children.

AMARANTH

Leaves of different varieties of the *amaranthus;* containing a proportionately large quantity of protein which is on the whole valuable and a small amount of carbohydrates; fairly rich in mineral elements; having large alkali excess; vitamin content unknown.

Amaranth leaves were widely used during the Middle Ages instead of spinach. The same good qualities are attributed to amaranth leaves as to spinach, but amaranth is more tender and has a milder taste.

APPLE

Fruit of the apple tree (*pyrus malus*); the fruits of the cultivated varieties are used almost exclusively, although those of the wild or crab apple tree are far more preferable from the nutrition standpoint. Being over-cultivated for thousands of years apples have improved only in appearance and taste; containing a slight alkali excess and only slight traces of the water-soluble vitamins B and C.

Because of its over-cultivation the value of the apple is usually overrated, nevertheless, it has many nutritive properties. Apples aid the digestion. Two apples, eaten before breakfast each morning, will help to overcome constipation because their fruit-acid salts stimulate the digestive processes and their semi-cellulose content softens the partly digested food in the large intestine. Fresh apple juice is also a great aid to digestion and most beneficial to those suffering from arthritic diseases and fevers. Apple juice should always be made from uncooked apples.

Many people believe that apples give them indigestion, but we have found no one who could not digest them once they got over this mistaken idea.

A delightful apple tea can be prepared from either fresh or dry apple parings. "Apple tea" has a pleasant aroma and can be used most advantageously as a substitute for Chinese tea.

APRICOT

Ripe fruit of the apricot tree (*prunus armeniaca*) often said to grow in Armenia, but in reality they originated in China; rich in potassium and iron; containing a high alkali excess; rich in water-soluble vitamins.

Ripe apricots are most delicious; unripe they

are bitter and most unappetizing and over-ripe they have a lush taste. In cases of liver or digestive disturbances apricots should always be cooked before eating. The Arabs use the fresh fruits as a cure for inflammation of the vocal cords and for diarrhea. On the other hand, dried, raw apricots that have been allowed to stand in water overnight act as a mild purgative. Eaten as dessert at the end of a meal, apricots are said to prevent flatulency (gas formation in the stomach).

ARTICHOKE

Scaly bud of the flowering head of a large thistle (*cynara scolymus*) gathered before the flower expands; very delicious after cooking; rich in potassium, sodium and calcium; being a bud vegetable, over-rich in phosphorus and sulphur acids and so having an acid excess; containing small proportion of water-soluble vitamins, and, strange to say, a fair quantity of the fat-soluble vitamin A; possessing an oxidizing ferment (*tyrosine*) and an insulin having the same properties.

All parts of the very tender, young artichoke heads can be eaten raw. The larger heads should be either steamed in a very small quantity of butter or thoroughly boiled in water to which a little salt has been added. When artichokes are cooked, only the fleshy portions, the soft base of the leaves of the flower, should be eaten, and the "choke" or scaly part thrown away. Artichokes are rich in tannic acid and, therefore, are slightly constipating. Also because of their high percentage of purine which tends to produce uric acid, artichokes are not to be recommended for diabetes. Unripe artichokes are said to be helpful to those who have jaundice, dropsy or rheumatism, and also to aid in increasing the activity of the liver; while the ripe vegetables are believed to stimulate the sexual organs. The water in which artichokes have been boiled has a strong diuretic action, but it is injurious in cases of kidney inflammation.

ARTICHOKE, JERUSALEM

Underground bulb of the *helianthus tuberosus;* containing fairly large amount of inferior protein and large quantities of carbohydrates, principally in the form of inulin; having large percentage of mineral substances; also large alkali excess; vitamin content unknown.

Formerly Jerusalem artichokes were very popular, but now they are used mostly as fodder for cattle. They have a somewhat sweetish taste like artichoke beans. These vegetables are prepared in the same ways as potatoes. Since inulin does not increase the sugar content in the blood, Jerusalem artichokes are recommended for diabetic patients as a substitute for potatoes.

ASPARAGUS

Underground sprouts as well as the "spears" or tips of the asparagus plant (*asparagus offici-*

nalis) ; very watery, very poor in nourishing elements; being a bud vegetable, over-rich in acids but containing an alkali excess; rich in an amino acid known as asparagine; little known about vitamin content.

Asparagus is said to act favorably upon the liver, bones, ligaments, skin and kidneys and to promote the formation of red blood corpuscles. This, however, is only superstition as when eaten excessively the action of asparagus upon the kidneys may prove injurious. Its assumed diuretic property does not increase the production of the urine, but only serves to irritate the bladder and kidneys which in the end causes an increased micturition (morbid desire to pass urine). Formerly asparagus was erroneously used for eczema and even for syphilis. Asparagus is still prescribed by many doctors for kidney diseases, but we most emphatically warn against it as it only tends to aggravate these complaints. Canned or preserved asparagus is more harmful than the fresh vegetable.

AVOCADO (ALLIGATOR PEARS)

Pulpy fruits of the lauraceous tree (*persea persea*) ; native to Persia but now growing wild in tropical America; fairly rich in potassium and sodium with small amounts of fluorine and iodine; rich in fat; containing large alkali excess; unknown vitamin content.

Avocado pears have a pleasant taste and are a valuable building food and an aid in overcoming constipation. They are also recommended to hasten delayed menstrual periods and to stimulate the sexual organs. Avocado pears have a laxative effect and serve to improve the appetite.

BACON

Fatty parts, especially the sides of the belly of the pig; consisting principally of fat; possessing a moderately high acid excess; having almost no water-soluble vitamins and only a small quantity of the fat-soluble vitamin A; containing small percentage of protein which is for the most part non-assimilable. For this reason bacon is the least injurious of all animal food products.

BAMBOO SHOOTS

Shoots of the different American bamboo species, while they are still white, especially the *phyllostachys* species; containing a fairly large amount of inferior protein, some carbohydrates and a small quantity of mineral elements; having small acid excess; vitamin content unknown.

Bamboo shoots are prepared for the table in the same way as asparagus.

BANANA

Fruit of the various varieties of a perennial, tree-like herb or banana plant (*musa sapientum, paradesiaca*, etc.); native of all tropical countries; rich in potassium, sodium and calcium; possessing an alkali excess; having a fair quantity of vitamin B and a large percentage of vitamin C, but very little of the fat-soluble vitamins; containing principally starches which as the fruits ripen are transformed into sugar, and also protein which appears to be incomplete. As a matter of fact in many tropical and sub-tropical countries they constitute almost the sole article of food. It is believed by some that bananas are constipating, but in reality, when not well chewed, they have a purgative effect.

Dried bananas, if they are not treated with sulphur acid make an excellent food which, unfortunately, is little known in America. Dried bananas make a splendid food for travelers, campers, and hunters. Children get much more benefit from fresh bananas than from candy or overly rich desserts. Because bananas are so satisfying and filling they should not be given to children between meals.

BARLEY

Ripe seeds of the barley grass (*hordium sativum*) of which there are many wild species which through cultivation have produced many other varieties; rich in potassium, silicic and phosphorus acids and sulphur; showing traces of iodine and fluorine; having high acid excess and almost none of the water-soluble vitamin B which is all concentrated in the pellicles (seed skins).

In Scotland and in other parts of Northern Europe barley is principally used in the making of bread. Unfortunately, by far the largest amount of the world's supply of barley is de-

voted to the brewing of beer, during which
process the nutritive elements are almost completely destroyed and transformed into alcohol.
Because of its strong acid excess barley should
only be eaten in small quantities and preferably
with fruits. Barley is considered to have both
a diuretic and "softening" effect. Therefore, it
is recommended to those who have some disease
of the respiratory organs which produces slime
or mucus. Evidently superstition alone ac-
counts for the fact that it is believed to cure
scrofula and cancer. Formerly, hot barley poul-
tices were often applied to parts of the body in
which pus was forming.

BEAN, ASPARAGUS

Young green pod and seeds of the *vigua
sesquipedalis;* containing moderately large
amount of fairly good protein; mineral element
content unknown; having small alkali excess.

Asparagus beans, like asparagus, are usually
cooked in a little salt water and eaten with butter. They have a strong diuretic action.

BEAN, FRESH STRING

Unripe pods of the *phaseolus vulgaris* and
nanus while they are still green; also an inferior variety (the wax bean) while the unripe
pods are still pale yellow; rich in potassium and
magnesium; having a rather small alkali excess;
containing fair proportions of all vitamins.

Unlike the green pods, the fully ripened pods are excellent for gout, kidney trouble, gallstones and rheumatism. They are especially beneficial when eaten with potatoes. The ripe, dry pods (husks) are said to contain an insulin of similar nature, but in this connection the exact contents appear to be very changeable. Extracts obtained by boiling the dry pods in water are recommended for diseases of the heart or kidneys and also for dropsy.

BEAN, KIDNEY

Seed of the *phaseolus vulgaris*, originally derived from the South American vegetable bean; more rare is the wood bean (*phaseolus nanus*) and the flower or fire bean (*phaseolus multiflorus*) varieties; very rich in protein which is, however, very inferior in quality; also very rich in fat and carbohydrates; rich is potassium, magnesium and phosphorus and sulphur acids; showing traces of iodine; having high acid excess and a large percentage of vitamin B, but only a small quantity of vitamin A and hardly any vitamin C.

Kidney beans are a highly concentrated food and, therefore, valuable, but should only be eaten in small quantities. The combination of beans with meat is altogether wrong. Because of their high acid content beans should always be eaten with vegetables, potatoes and fruits. Those who have gout or kidney trouble should never include them in their diet.

BEAN, LIMA

Seed of the *phaseolus lunatus* and *macrocarpus;* rich in incomplete protein and carbohydrates; containing, however, a glucoside which when it comes in contact with water produces prussic acid; composition of mineral elements unknown; having acid excess; vitamin content unknown.

Baked lima beans should now and then be used as a meat substitute.

BEAN, SOYA

Seed derived from *soja hispida.* These beans, which are cultivated in the countries of Japan and China, play a most important part in the diet of their people. Within the last few years the soya bean has also been cultivated in America, and, because they contain so many healthful properties, are bound to become a popular food. They are the only legumes which contain a complete and valuable protein, such as we find in milk or meat; and also contain a valuable fat, but no carbohydrates. Preparation should be in the same manner as navy beans, but they must be cooked longer. Soya bean flour may be added to whole wheat flour to make a delicious and healthful bread. There are soya bean extracts on the market, which are used chiefly by the Japanese and Chinese. These extracts are alkaline forming and should also be used by Americans in place of the acid-forming meat extracts.

BEEF

Flesh of the domestic heifer or steer; rich in calcium and sodium; but still richer in phosphorus and sulphur acids; having high acid excess; containing small percentage of vitamin B, even smaller amount of vitamin A and no trace of vitamin C.

Meat contains a so-called meat alkali, but is composed principally of protein and fat. It is a good protein-supplying food. Eating beef regularly in large quantities is a bad habit, as beef contains too much acid-forming protein and so may destroy the necessary alkali excess in the body. Beef should be procured only from young cattle, preferably from grass-fed animals and should always be eaten with vegetables and fruits. It is best to abstain from beef altogether in nearly all illnesses, in fact, it is inadvisable to each much meat at any time.

Dried meat is highly but erroneously recommended for those who wish to reduce because some of the high protein content changes into fat in the process of digestion.

BEET, RED

Swollen top root of a special variety of *beta vulgaris* of the *rapa forma rubra*, containing small amount of incomplete protein; rich in sugar, potassium and sodium; having alkali excess and slight percentage of vitamin B.

Either raw or cooked beets are excellent vegetables especially for salads. When eaten raw they must first be mashed or shredded. Beets have a soothing effect upon the nerves and help the liver to function properly. Because of their bright red color they were once thought to aid in the production of healthy blood, but this is an entirely fallacious belief.

BEET, SUGAR

Swollen top root of a special cultivated variety of beets used for animal fodder (*beta altessima*); containing incomplete protein, a plentiful amount of cellulose and cane-sugar; rich in potassium and calcium; having alkali excess; rich in vitamin B; possessing small quantity of vitamin C; containing also an oxidizing ferment which when in contact with the air changes the tyrosine (amino-acid) found in the juice into a black insoluble powder.

Sugar beets are as a general rule cooked with a bit of sugar. They are most beneficial when eaten raw in salads. The fresh juice of sugar beets is sometimes thought to be a remedy for all kinds of tumors, even cancer, but this idea is in all probability just another superstition.

BLACKBERRY

Black fruit of several *rubus* varieties, especially the *rubus fructicosus* and *caesius*; rich in sugar, aromatic ingredients and cellulose; also rich in organic acids, potassium and calcium; containing fairly high alkali excess; rich in vitamin B; having small percentage of vitamin C.

Blackberries are excellent fruits from the nutrition standpoint and have a strong, aromatic flavor. Many people can not digest the seeds. In such cases the seeds should be bitten into tiny pieces by the teeth or else the berries should be thoroughly chewed and the seeds removed from the mouth as many people do when eating grapes. At one time blackberries were supposed to cause headache and fever, but this idea was erroneous. Also it was believed that because of their red juice they supplied red blood corpuscles, but this also is not true. Blackberry juice is a good remedy for fever, gout and diarrhea. The raw berries contain cane-sugar and are, therefore, used in reducing diets.

BLOOD

Derived from the cow and pig; principally used as a food in preference to mutton, etc.; very rich in valuable protein; pig's blood containing some fat; rich in minerals; especially rich in potassium and phosphorus acid; having small alkali excess and slight amount of vitamins A and B.

Blood is preferable to meat because it does not contain so many stimulating elements. Judged from the ethical viewpoint, blood is a distasteful food since it involves drawing the life blood from a living animal for one's own nourishment. Blood is especially to be recommended in cases where the patient is suffering from a deficiency of red blood corpuscles or the disease known as anemia. In Northern Europe *blood bread* is much esteemed. This "bread" is made by mixing blood, flour and fat. Cooking changes this mixture into a solid loaf which is then cut into slices, fried in fat and eaten with fruits.

BLUEBERRY

Ripe fruit of the *myrtillus niger;* containing small amount of incomplete protein and fair amount of tannin and pectin; rich in potassium; having great alkali excess; fairly rich in vitamin B; possessing small proportion of vitamin C.

Blueberries were once a very popular remedy. Because of the tannic acid they contain, they are most beneficial in treating diarrhea, dysentery and intestinal bleeding. They are also said to reduce the sugar secretion in diabetes. Blueberry juice is rich in antiseptic properties and has a depressing effect.

BRAIN

Derived from various kinds of animals that nourish their young with milk; very rich in protein and fat and also in phosphorus-rich ingredients such as lecithin, cerasin and cholesterin; very rich in potassium and an organic combination of phosphorus and sulphur; having high acid excess; containing fair amount of vitamin B and small percentage of vitamin A.

Brain is a highly concentrated food which should be eaten in small quantities. It has been recommended for nervous diseases, but wrongly so. It is particularly injurious to those suffering from diabetes, tuberculosis or kidney diseases.

BRAZIL NUT

Large, hard-shelled nut of a South American tree (*bertholletia excelsa*); rich in incomplete protein, fat and starches; also rich in potassium; exceedingly rich in calcium and phosphorus; containing high acid excess; having fair proportion of vitamin B and traces of vitamins A and C.

Brazil nuts constitute a valuable food, but on account of their rich protein content they should be eaten sparingly and then thoroughly chewed. Otherwise, they are likely to irritate the very sensitive lining of the intestinal tract.

BREAD, RYE, WHOLE

Made from the flour of the complete seeds of rye-grass and Secale cereal (cultivated rye): fairly rich in incomplete protein and in fat; very rich in starches; rich in potassium and phosphorus and sulphur acids; having high acid excess and fair amount of vitamin B. Whole rye bread is often considered hard to digest. This, however, is not true. If the flour is ground sufficiently fine whole rye bread is as easy to digest as fine white bread. At one time wheat protein was considered the most valuable grain protein, but recent experiments have proved that rye protein is actually more beneficial.

BREAD, WHEAT, WHOLE

Made from the ground whole grains of the wheat grass; fairly rich in inferior protein, also in fat and starches; rich in potassium and phosphorus and sulphur acids; having fairly large acid excess; possessing small percentage of vitamin B.

The protein content in whole wheat bread is inferior to that in whole rye bread.

BREAD, WHITE

Made from refined grains of the wheat grass; fairly rich in protein and fat; very rich in starches; moderately rich in potassium; rich in phosphorus and sulphur acids; possessing acid excess; containing hardly any vitamins.

White bread has little food value. It is only suitable for people suffering from gout and this only because it contains less acid than whole wheat bread.

BREAD, GRAHAM

Made from the husks and entire crushed kernels of the rye-grass (*hordeum sativum*).

Graham bread is very difficult to digest because it irritates the intestines. Therefore, it should not be eaten by those who have sensitive or diseased digestive tracts.

BROCCOLI

A variety of the common cauliflower derived from the *brassica oleracea asparagoides*; the edible parts being the fleshy stalks and pollen; rich in potassium; containing fair proportions of phosphorus and sulphur acids and traces of iodine; having alkali excess; rich in vitamin B; possessing small percentage of vitamin C.

Broccoli is a beneficial food, especially to be recommended to those wishing to reduce.

BRUSSELS SPROUT

Bud of a cultivated variety of the common cabbage plant (*brassica oleracea gemmifera*); comparatively rich in incomplete protein; containing almost twice as much protein as any other kind of cabbage; rich in cellulose, potassium and phosphorus acid; above all rich in sulphur acid; having fairly high alkali excess; vitamin content unknown. Brussels sprouts are one of the few bud vegetables that contain sulphur acid, therefore, they are decidedly less valuable as a food than the other varieties of cabbage. When eaten raw brussels sprouts have an unpleasant taste and so it is best to boil them or to steam them in fat.

BUCKWHEAT

Ripe seed grains of the *fagopyrum esculentum,* a species of knot-grass native to Central Asia which has now spread over the Northern Hemisphere; containing a fairly small amount of incomplete protein and a small quantity of fat; rich in carbohydrates; also rich in potassium and very rich in phosphorus and sulphur acids; having a large acid excess; vitamin content unknown. In the United States buckwheat ground into meal or flour is used principally for pancakes. It can not be used alone in baked breads, but must be supplemented by other kinds of flour. Buckwheat has a somewhat bitter taste, but nevertheless has a better flavor than millet. Owing to the fact that buckwheat is poor in fat and has an excess of acid, pancakes or breads, made of buckwheat, should be eaten together with some fatty food and plenty of vegetables and fruits. Buckwheat is particularly recommended for lymphatic diseases.

BURDOCK

Roots of the burdock varieties especially the *arctium lappa;* containing a fairly large amount of inferior protein and large quantities of carbohydrates, cellulose and inulin; mineral element content unknown; having alkali excess; vitamin content unknown. These roots were formerly eaten in the same way as carrots. The young stalks and roots of the burdock varieties can also be used as a vegetable and to put in soups. They were at one time popular as a medicine.

BUTTER

Unmelted fat extracted from milk; composed for the most part of fat; in general containing few minerals; possessing acid surplus; rich in vitamin A; having in summer also some vitamin D.

Owing to the fact that butter contains a very small percentage of melted fat, of all fats it is the easiest to digest. After butter has been melted, its natural consistency is lost and then it is about as easy to digest as mineral oil. From the ethical standpoint, butter is the best animal fat.

The composition and food value of butter varies a great deal according to the season and the fodder on which the cows are fed. The best butter is produced from the milk of pasture-fed cows and the least beneficial from artificially fed cattle. Cows that are always kept in the stalls and given only dry fodder produce milk very deficient in vitamins. Milk is most healthful when raw or certified.

BUTTERNUT

Large, nut-like seed of the *caryocar butyrosum* and others of the same variety from Brazil and Guiana; rich in protein; very rich in fat and carbohydrates; rich in potassium, magnesium and phosphorus acid; having acid excess; vitamin content unknown. Butternuts are a concentrated food which because of their acid excess should always be eaten with fruits.

CABBAGE, RED

Variety of the *brassica oleracea capitata* with red leaves; having the same composition as white cabbage.

The properties and food value of red cabbage

are identical with those of white cabbage, but the red cabbage has a much tougher leaf. Red cabbage can also be pickled and then it resembles sauerkraut. During this pickling process the red coloring matter or pigment changes to a lighter shade through the action of the acids. Red cabbage becomes purple when boiled.

Because of its sulphur content all cabbage is said to tend to produce flatulency. There is some truth in this assertion, but by careful preparation it is possible to avoid this disadvantage. While the cabbage is boiling the lid of the pot should be raised from time to time and the sulphurous water shaken off the inside of the cover, or else the vegetable should be cut in finger slices and fried in a hot pan, without the addition of butter or fat, until they are well browned on both sides. In this way the flatulent elements are removed. Only after frying, if desired, should water or fat be added, and then the cabbage is ready to serve. Also, to avoid gas formation, cabbage should always be thoroughly chewed.

Owing to its sulphur content, too, raw cabbage should be eaten most sparingly by those suffering from kidney diseases. For such persons it is advisable that cabbage be either boiled or fried by the methods explained above.

CABBAGE, SPROUT

Sprout growing on the green cabbage stalks after the cabbages have been cut from their stalks in the springtime; containing small amount of incomplete protein, some carbohydrates and a great deal of cellulose; having a large proportion of potassium, and, depending upon age, either an alkali or acid excess, the more tender they are the smaller the alkali content; fairly rich in vitamin B.

Cabbage sprouts are delicious and tender, however, they should always be eaten with potatoes.

CABBAGE, WHITE

Unopened heads of the white cabbage plant (*brassica oleracea capitata*); having small and inferior protein content and small percentage of sugar; rich in potassium and calcium; containing fairly large alkali excess and traces of iodine: raw cabbage, rich in all water-soluble vitamins and in vitamin A; also containing small quantity of vitamin D: cooked cabbage, still retaining a large amount of vitamin A and a fair quantity of the water-soluble vitamins.

White cabbage is one of our most healthful vegetables and should preferably be eaten raw. It is particularly effective in overcoming constipation.

CABBAGE, WHITE (SAUERKRAUT)

White cabbage cut fine and fermented in lactic acid bacilli (brine made from its own juice with salt added); having same composition as white cabbage; especially rich in vitamin C. Sauerkraut possesses all the healthful properties of white cabbage, and because of its acid content it has a strong, stimulating effect upon the digestive organs. For this reason it is particularly recommended for sluggish intestines and constipation. Those who are unable to digest sauerkraut will obtain beneficial results from drinking sauerkraut juice which is also prescribed for diabetes. Raw sauerkraut is also a valuable food. Raw sauerkraut served with onions and cream or lemon juice is particularly palatable. The juice must be eaten with it and, therefore, the raw kraut should not be washed before eating. It is also a mistake to add flour to sauerkraut.

CAKES

Made from refined flour with a little sugar and some condiment added; having small amount of inferior protein; containing mostly starches; generally deficient in mineral substances, having acid excess and practically no vitamins.

CARROT

Cultivated variety of the *daucus carota* which was long used as a food by the peasantry; containing inferior protein; rich in carbohydrates, potassium, sodium and calcium; having high alkali excess, a trace of iodine and a fair proportion of all the vitamins.

After cooking, carrots have a smaller percentage of the water-soluble vitamins. They are most beneficial when eaten raw, but should be well chewed. When cooking carrots, and this applies in general to all vegetables, the water in which they have been boiled should not be thrown away because this water contains the most valuable ingredients. The real significance of carrots as a health food is not yet fully known. Owing to their abundance in the fat-soluble vitamins, the fresh juice of carrots, added to an infant's milk, prevents rickets and removes the necessity of having to resort to dangerous drug preparations. Carrot juice also constitutes a powerful cleansing and acid-neutralizing food for adults. Carrots contain an insulin-like ingredient and a hormone-like ferment called tokokinin. This is probably the reason why diabetics digest the sugar in carrots more easily than any other kind of sugar. The housewife also knows that the delicate green leaves of the carrot make an especially appetizing dish.

CAROB

Ripe pod of the Saint-John's-bread or carob-bean (*ceratonia siliquosa*) native to countries on the Mediterranean Sea; having small amount of inferior protein and some sugar; rich in potassium, calcium and phosphorus acid with traces of iodine; vitamin content unknown.

Carob pods are chiefly used as a food in Asia and North Africa where they are usually baked into hot cakes. Also they are often separated from their kernels, ground and then baked with pea flour or groats (dried grain, hulled and crushed). When the kernels are eaten with the pods carob has a high acid excess; while the pods without the kernels have a strong alkali excess. A syrup made from carob pods is most efficacious in cases of violent diarrhea, provided that the syrup is made from the dried pods as the fresh ones have a slight laxative action. Carob pods are also recommended for inflammation of the respiratory organs.

CATSUP, TOMATO

Acid relish obtained principally from tomatoes, which, however, should be sparingly used.

CAULIFLOWER

Stalk and flower-bud of the *brassica oleracea cauliflora;* having small amount of inferior protein; fairly rich in sugar; very rich in loose cellulose; rich in potassium and calcium; containing a fair quantity of mustard oil, fair amount of vitamin B and small percentages of vitamins A and C.

Because cauliflower causes a slight flatulency it should be steamed or boiled in an open pan. Also since the mustard oil in this vegetable tends to irritate the kidneys, those suffering from kidney diseases should eat only small amounts of it.

CAVIAR

Eggs of the sturgeon species of fish; rich in valuable protein; containing some fat; rich in potassium, calcium and phosphorus and sulphur;

possessing high acid excess, moderate quantity of vitamin B and small amount of vitamin A.

Caviar is also derived from many other fish besides the sturgeon, especially from the haddock and salmon species. The Zoroastrian sect claim that even the most strict vegetarian may eat caviar because its production does not necessitate the death of the fish. This, however, is not the case as caviar is cut from the stomach of the fish after it is dead. Caviar is not an economical food and furthermore is dangerous because the fish are to a great extent infested with parasites that frequently lodge themselves in the ovaries of the fish. Because it is so easily assimilated, caviar is recommended in some cases of indigestion. It would be preferable, however, to follow a more natural diet to remedy these faulty conditions of the digestion.

CEDAR NUT

Nut of various species of the fir and pine trees; rich in incomplete protein, tannic acid, potassium, sodium and calcium; very rich in phosphorus and sulphur acids; having, therefore, a very high acid excess; containing only small amounts of vitamins A and B. The kernels of cedar nuts can be eaten raw, but are more often roasted. In the Mediterranean countries they are mixed with sugar and made into nougat candy. At one time they were prescribed in cases of consumption, and they are actually beneficial to

those who have catarrh because they free the
air passages. The nutritive value of these nuts,
which properly speaking do not come under the
classification of nuts, still remains doubtful on
account of their high protein and consequent
acid content.

CELERY, BLEACHED

Stalks of the celery plant (*apium graveolens*)
growing under the surface of the ground; having
a slight amount of incomplete protein and some
sugar; rich in potassium, sodium and calcium;
possessing high alkali excess; vitamin content
unknown.

Celery is best eaten raw. It has a decidedly
beneficial effect upon the entire nervous system,
and was recommended by Hippocrates for the
treatment of nervous complaints. Raw celery
juice is also used successfully for gout and various other forms of rheumatism.

CELERY LEAVES

Green leaves of the celery plant growing in
the daylight above the surface of the ground;
containing a little more incomplete protein and
more sugar than the bleached celery; rich in
potassium and sodium; particularly rich in sulphur acid; having high alkali excess; rich in
vitamins A and B, apparently also in C; containing an ingredient of insulin and a ferment known
as tokokinin.

Celery leaves may be eaten raw, but when

this is done, on account of their toughness, it is advisable to chop them. They may also be boiled. Because of their very strong taste they are best used as a condiment or as an addition to the cooked stalks. Celery leaves are very beneficial, especially raw, for nervous disorders, gout and all other acid conditions. Because of their insulin content, the raw leaves of the celery plant are excellent for treating diabetes.

CELERY ROOT

Fully developed root of the celery plant; having a small amount of incomplete protein and a fair proportion of sugar; rich in potassium and sodium; very rich in calcium; possessing high alkali excess; containing large amount of vitamin B and small percentage of vitamin A. Celery roots, owing to their hardness and toughness, when eaten raw must first be grated. In this grated form they are particularly helpful in curing nervous disorders and dropsy.

CHARD

Leaves and leaf stalk of the common beet (*beta vulgaris*); containing a small amount of incomplete protein and some carbohydrates; having a plentiful quantity of potassium and some calcium; possessing a high alkali excess; rich in vitamin B.

CHERRY

Fruit of various species of the *prunus* tree of which there are a number of cultivated varieties;

deficient in incomplete protein; fairly rich in sugar and organic fruit acids; rich in potassium; containing fairly large alkali excess; rich in vitamin B; possessing small amount of vitamin C.

The sour varieties of cherries are used in reducing diets; while the very sweet varieties are to be recommended to those who wish to increase their weight. Sour cherries should be eaten before meals as an appetizer; sweet cherries after meals as a dessert. Cherries, eaten in sufficient quantities (about a pound a day) tend to regulate the eliminative process of the intestines. They greatly stimulate the secretion of the urine and do so without injury to the kidneys. Cherries are also helpful in cases of hardening of the arteries. When cherries are preserved, canned or bottled, very often the stones are not removed. Care should be taken in this respect since cherry stones contain prussic acid.

CHERVIL

Leaves of the *anthriscus cerefolium;* containing fairly large amount of valuable protein, also fairly large quantity of carbohydrates and large proportion of ethereal oil; having large amount of mineral substances and alkali excess; vitamin content unknown. Because of its strong taste chervil is for the most part used as a flavoring ingredient for other vegetables, fruits and salads. It is said to stimulate the activity of the liver; to have a diuretic effect; to hasten retarded menstruation; to decrease the supply of mother's milk and to loosen phlegm.

CHESTNUT

Nut of the chestnut tree (*castanea vesca*); fairly rich in incomplete protein and in fat; very rich in carbohydrates; also very rich in potassium, sodium and magnesium; possessing an acid excess resulting from its richness in sulphur and phosphorus; containing only a small amount of vitamin B.

Because of their tannic acid content chestnuts should not be eaten raw. Also because of the toughness of their fibre, unless thoroughly chewed, they are very indigestible. These nuts are usually boiled or roasted before eating. They can serve as a substitute for potatoes and may also be used in bread making. On account of their excess acid content, however, if eaten in large quantities they are likely to cause acidity of the stomach.

COLLARDS: See KALE

COTTAGE CHEESE

Curdled and compressed casein (white, crumbling substance of acid character) in milk; rich in protein and, varying with the recipe, rich in fat; also rich in calcium and phosphorus and sulphur acids; usually having strong salt content; possessing high acid excess and only a small amount of vitamins A and B. Cottage cheese is a very satisfying and valuable food product. Because of its rich protein content and acid excess, it should always be eaten together with fresh fruit. Cottage cheese and pineapple make a very healthful combination. Cottage cheese has a constipating tendency.

CHEESE, GOAT

Made from goat's milk; rich in protein and fat; also rich in potassium, calcium and phosphorus and sulphur acids; having large acid excess and small amount of vitamin A.

This cheese is a good protein food product, which should, however, only be eaten in small quantities. Roquefort cheese (made from the milk of ewes with cow's milk sometimes added) may be included in this category. It derives its pleasant taste from the green mold produced on the cheese during the process of manufacture. Contrary to others, this cheese, when eaten moderately, has a slight purgative effect.

CHEESE, SWISS, AND OTHER SIMILAR VARIETIES

Through the *schizomycetes* (mixed bacteria) of its changing casein and according to the recipe used, this cheese is very rich in protein and also in fat; rich in potassium; very rich in calcium and phosphorus and sulphur acids; having acid excess and a small amount of vitamin A.

Swiss cheese is a very nutritious and satisfying protein food product and should, therefore, be eaten moderately. It is slightly constipating in its effect.

CHICK PEAS

Ripe fruits of the *cicer arietinum;* rich in incomplete protein; very rich in fat and cellulose; rich in potassium and phosphorus and sulphur acids; having acid excess and fair amount of vitamin B with traces of vitamin A.

Chick peas are a coarse, indigestible food which produce a large amount of gas in the stomach. They are said to be stimulating to the sexual organs, but this is just superstition. They do, however, have a strong diuretic action. Like all pod vegetables, chick peas, eaten to excess, cause kidney stones.

CHICORY

Root of the common chicory plant (*cichorium intybus*) which have been bleached by the exclusion of all light; having a small amount of incomplete protein; rich in potassium; possessing alkali excess; vitamin content unknown.

Chicory, according to a long-standing belief, is an aid to digestion and a successful remedy for liver complaints. On account of its bitter ingredients, chicory stimulates the appetite. It has a strong diuretic action and is also beneficial in such diseases as gout and dropsy. Chicory is best eaten raw or cooked in butter. Chicory roots should never be cooked in water as water gives them a very bitter taste. For this reason

they should not even be washed before cooking.
Formerly these roots were eaten just as we eat
carrots today. Now they are for the most part
roasted and used as a coffee substitute.

CHIVES

Green leaves of the *allium schoenoprasum;*
comparatively rich in protein and fat; rich in
potassium and calcium; having rich alkali excess
and fair amounts of vitamins B and C.

Chives aid in dissolving the phlegm in catarrh
and in stimulating the appetite. They also help
to secrete the gastric juices by stimulating the
digestive organs, and exercise a strong diuretic
action. Because of the large amount of mustard
oil contained in chives, they should not be eaten
in large quantities by those who have kidney
diseases. Chives make an especially delicious
condiment for salads. Also owing to their strong
diuretic action it is commonly believed that these
vegetables are particularly beneficial as a blood
cleanser.

CHOCOLATE

A mixture of sugar and cocoa to which some
other ingredient such as vanilla, etc., is usually
added; rich in incomplete protein, starches and
fat; also rich in potassium, calcium and phosphorus and sulphur acids; containing acid excess
and hardly any vitamins. Chocolate, being a
concentrated food product with a high acid ex-

cess, should only be eaten in small quantities. It contains an alkaloid, similar to that found in caffeine, called theobroma, from which it derives its stimulating properties. Theobroma, however, is comparatively non-poisonous. Chocolate is a very constipating food, and has a tendency to cause the rapid decay of the teeth because the fine chocolate grains secrete themselves in the cavities of the tooth enamel. It should be remembered, too, that chocolate is a very fattening food.

CIDER

Fermented apple juice; having as its principal ingredients alcohol and some sugar; rich in fruit acids; very poor in mineral substances; possessing a small alkali excess and hardly any vitamins.

Apple cider is recommended as an appetizer and as an aid to digestion, but the apple juice is decidedly more beneficial when it is taken in its original, unfermented state.

COCOA

Fermented, partially ripe seeds of the cocoa tree (*theobroma cacao*) after they have been roasted, shelled and finely ground; rich in incomplete protein, starches and fat; very rich in potassium and calcium; rich in phosphorus and sulphur acids; containing high acid excess and small amount of vitamin B.

Cocoa, like chocolate, has a stimulating effect

and is also fattening. It, too, has a tendency to cause slight constipation.

COCOANUT

Fruit of the cocoa palm (*cocos nucifera*) ; rich in protein and fat; having small amount of carbohydrates; very rich in cellulose; rich in potassium and phosphorus and sulphur acids; containing some acid excess and a fair amount of vitamins A and B. Cocoanuts are a very nutritious food which, however, must be well chewed or they will prove indigestible. Because of their rich protein and fat content they are very fattening. In the tropics they are used as a remedy for liver and stomach disorders and are also believed to destroy "worms," meaning parasitic worms which sometimes lodge in the intestines.

COFFEE

Dried and roasted kernels from the coffee bean; derived from various species of the coffee tree (*coffea arabica, etc.*) ; very rich in the stimulating alkaloid, caffeine; containing hardly anything else but taste ingredients.

Coffee can be prepared by boiling the finely ground kernels in an ordinary coffee pot. When a percolator, tricolator or drip pot is used the boiling water pours through the grounds. Preparation by the drip method is the least harmful, since coffee is most injurious when the grounds have been allowed to stand in the water.

Strong coffee causes palpitation of the heart

and insomnia. When regularly consumed in large quantities it produces a highly undesirable nervous condition. For this reason it is not well to drink coffee at a late hour.

COLA

Dried kernels of the cola tree; rich in incomplete protein and carbohydrates; also rich in potassium, calcium and phosphorus and sulphur acids; having acid excess and small quantities of vitamins A and B.

Cola nuts are really more of a stimulant than a food. They are fairly rich in caffeine and, therefore, have the same effect upon the system as coffee. The reputation of this product has been greatly injured by the report that more people in Northern Europe and also in North America and England have been caffeine-poisoned by cola nut fountain drinks than by coffee itself.

A little cola nut eaten or imbibed as a beverage on long, tiresome journeys has a refreshing, stimulating effect, but the long continued use of cola nuts is harmful.

CORN

Ripe seeds of the *zea maydis* in different varieties, both yellow and white; comparatively rich in very incomplete protein; rich in carbohydrates and fat; rich in potassium and phosphorus and sulphur acids; having acid excess and very small amount of any kind of vitamin. (Vitamin A is

found in the yellow corn and so also is a fluo-
renic dye or coloring ingredient formed by ex-
posure to the sun which produces severe skin
eruptions in people who are susceptible.)

White corn is not only inferior, but also very
indigestible. Corn and corn meal are thought by
the majority to be excellent foods, but this is
not true. Corn is the least nutritious of all
grains. An almost exclusive diet of corn, because of its lack of anti-pellegra vitamins, will
bring on that terrible disease, pellegra.

CORN MEAL, MAIZE

Finest sifted flour derived from fully ripe
corn; containing incomplete protein, some fat
and a large quantity of starch; fairly rich in
potassium and phosphorus and sulphur acids;
having acid excess and practically no vitamin
content.

Maize corn meal is a very inferior food.

CORN-ON-COB

Unripe fruit stalk of the corn plant, while the
seeds are still milky; containing small amount
of incomplete protein; rich in sugar; also rich
in potassium and phosphorus acid; having an
alkali excess, growing less as the seeds ripen until
it is finally transformed into an acid excess; comparatively rich in vitamin B. Corn-on-cob is
most nourishing when the cobs are young and
small. Later they acquire the same properties as
the ripe seeds described above. Those who wish

to reduce should avoid corn altogether as it has a decided fattening tendency.

COW PEAS

Fresh, ripe seeds of the Chinese pea (*vignea sinensis*); containing fairly large amount of incomplete protein and a large quantity of starch; having small acid excess; vitamin content unknown.

CRAB MEAT

Meat of the small crab (*astacus fluviatilis*); rich in protein, but fairly deficient in fat. (At certain times of the year, however, rich fat substances are found in the body and especially under the shell and on the breast of the crab.) Rich in potassium, sodium and phosphorus and sulphur acids; containing relatively large amount of iodine; having strong acid excess and some vitamin B.

Crab meat is a dainty dish, but, owing to its high protein and sulphur acid contents, it should be eaten with caution.

CRACKERS

Generally made from refined wheat flour, using a drying process. The composition and food value of crackers are the same as those of wheat bread.

CRACKER, SODA

This cracker counteracts acidity of the stomach, but, because of its sole contribution of sodium ingredients, it tends to aggravate the disease and lengthen its cure.

CRACKER, SWEDISH

Generally made from rye corn flour, thoroughly baked in a flat, pancake-like loaf; comparatively rich in protein; very rich in starches and dextrin; having small amount of fat; rich in potassium; comparatively rich in calcium; containing too much magnesium; possessing large quantities of phosphorus and sulphur acids and some iodine and fluorine; having a strong acid excess. Swedish bread is the most nourishing of breads.

CRANBERRY

Ripe fruit of the *vaccinium vitio idaea;* poor in protein; fairly rich in organic acids, especially in tannic acid; rich in potassium; very rich in sulphur acid; having acid excess; rich in vitamin B; containing small proportion of vitamin C. People in the Northern countries are very fond of cranberries. Due to their high percentage of sulphur, cranberries, chemically speaking, have an acid excess. Nevertheless, it would seem that this sulphur is an integral part of the pigment or coloring of the berries and leaves the actual chemistry of the berries as food unchanged. Cranberries do not appear to cause acidity, but seem to have an alkalizing effect. This explains why they are used as a household remedy for various diseases, especially gout, and are frequently prescribed for diabetes. They are most beneficial for diarrhea. When eaten raw they are valuable in stopping fever. Cranberries stimulate the liver, but they are not very efficacious in kidney diseases.

CREAM

Rich, oily, yellowish part of milk, which gradually rises and collects on the surface of milk; containing a small amount of complete protein; having very small percentage of milk-sugar; rich in fat; also rich in potassium; very rich in calcium and phosphorus and sulphur acids, resulting in small acid excess; possessing large amount of vitamin A and small proportion of vitamin B; cream from the milk of pasture-fed cows also containing some vitamin D.

Cream is a very nutritious food. Because of its fat content cream should be avoided by stout people and those who wish to reduce.

CRESS, WATER

Leaves and young shoots of the *lepidium sativum*; containing fairly large amount of protein, small quantity of carbohydrates and relatively large proportion of mustard oil; having alkali excess; vitamin content unknown.

Water cress is an excellent salad food, but it has so strong a taste that it is best mixed with other salad ingredients. Since it contains mustard oil, those suffering from kidney diseases should abstain from it.

CUCUMBER

Fruit of the different varieties of the *curcuma sativa*; having a small protein content and a fair amount of sugar and cellulose; very rich in sodium, calcium and magnesium; also rich in phosphorus and sulphur acids; containing an alkali excess; very rich in vitamin C, and having a small amount of vitamin B.

Cucumbers are an excellent food and are stimulating and easily digested whether boiled, stewed or baked. They are generally eaten far too infrequently and then only as a salad with the addition of too much mustard or vinegar. The best way to prepare cucumbers in salad form is to cut the unpeeled vegetables into very thin slices, and then add a small amount of lemon juice and oil or sour cream. Cucumbers may also be salted or pickled, but lose much of their food value.

Cucumbers have a diuretic action without injuring the kidneys or the gall bladder. They are also excellent in cases of gout and all other metabolic diseases. Fresh cucumber juice has a stimulating effect on the skin when it is rubbed on at night and allowed to dry.

CURDS; CURD CHEESE

Fresh curdled casein from which the water has been removed, obtained from the natural souring or the renneting of milk; consisting principally of protein; containing more or less fat, depending upon whether it is made from whole or skimmed milk; very rich in potassium and calcium; fairly rich in sodium and in phosphorus and sulphur acids and in chlorine; having strong acid excess and traces of vitamin B; showing also traces of vitamin A when made from whole milk.

Curds are the best protein-supplying food, but precisely on that account and also because of their excess acid content, they should be eaten only in small quantities; one or two spoonfuls at a time being sufficient.

CURRANT

Ripe fruit of the different *ribes* varieties, especially the black and red types; containing small quantity of incomplete protein; much sugar and a large amount of fruit juices; rich in potassium; having alkali excess and fair quantity of vitamin B and some of vitamin C.

Currants are very refreshing fruits. Their juice is especially beneficial in cases of stomach or intestinal catarrh. It is popularly believed that currants have blood-forming properties. They are decidedly helpful in lowering a fever and in stimulating the salivary glands, and are also beneficial in treating kidney or stomach diseases, and apparently also heart diseases.

Black currants are used as a sudorific (perspiration inducing) remedy and although they are rich in tannic acid, they are useful in overcoming intestinal catarrh, and for this purpose only the juice should be used.

DANDELION GREEN

Tender green leaf of the young dandelion plants (*taraxacum officinalis*) ; containing small amount of valuable protein; having some tannic acid and bitter ingredients; (when fully developed the leaves become tough and contain some caoutchouc or rubber) ; very rich in potassium, calcium, sodium and phosphorus acid; possessing high alkali excess; fairly rich in vitamin B; very rich in vitamins A, C and D.

Dandelion greens are one of the most delicious of spring vegetables. The old leaves are, as a rule, too bitter for the average taste, but by removing the tough middle rib of the leaf they may be used as an addition to other vegetable dishes. They make a splendid appetizer. These greens stimulate the glands, especially the liver and cause a copious flow of bile and act as a strong urine dissolvent. For this reason they were at one time prescribed for dropsy. In cases of eczema the eating of raw dandelion greens is said to have brought about excellent results. These greens have even been recommended as beneficial in cancerous conditions.

The roasted roots of the dandelion are used as a coffee substitute, but the taste of "dandelion coffee" is too bitter to be entirely pleasing. This "coffee" is also said to be beneficial in the diseases mentioned above. There are many green plants similar to dandelions which are equally delicious, nutritious and curative.

DATE

Ripe fruit of the date palm (*phoenix dactylifera*) and other varieties containing fair amount of inferior protein; very rich in sugar and cellulose; also very rich in potassium; proportionately rich in sodium, calcium and magnesium; rich in sulphur acid and chlorine; having alkali excess and some vitamin B.

Dates reach us only in the dried state. Because the light varieties of dates are often treated with sulphuric acid and so have a decidedly acid content, the dark varieties, not so treated, are much to be preferred. Dates are excellent fruits because they supply bulk which promotes peristaltic action, or, the mechanical function of the intestinal muscles. Dates are also said to act favorably upon the nervous system and to aid in curing catarrh. A thick syrup made from dates will loosen the phlegm in catarrhal conditions. If eaten in sufficient quantities just before retiring dates will induce sleep. Dates will also relieve children who suffer from diarrhea. Most children are very fond of dates and their taste should be gratified as dates are certainly a most healthful substitute for candy.

DEER

Flesh of the different *cervus* varieties; for composition and properties see BEEF. The only difference between deer and beef being that deer is more lean and more difficult to digest.

DILL

Leaves and budding flowers of the dill plant (*anethum graveolens*); proportionately rich in complete protein, carbohydrates and cellulose; very rich in ethereal oils; rich in potassium, sodium, calcium and phosphorus and sulphur acids and chlorine; having strong alkali excess; rich in vitamin B; also in A and C.

Because of its strong odor, the dill can be used only as a pickle. It is said to have both stimulating and gas-expelling properties. The dill is believed to increase the secretion of mother's milk as well as to loosen the phlegm in cases of colds or coughs. It is a food remedy for stomach aches, flatulency or gas, menstrual disorders and the vomiting which often occurs during the first few months of pregnancy. Owing to the large percentage of ethereal oil which it contains, dill should never be eaten by those who have kidney trouble.

DOCK: See SORREL

DUCK

Flesh of the various duck species; rich in protein; fairly rich in fat, which furthermore is somewhat strong in flavor; rich in potassium and sodium; very rich in phosphorus and sulphur acids; having acid excess and small amount of vitamin B.

The meat of wild ducks is tougher than that

of the domesticated fowl. In general, duck meat may be said to be as nutritious as that of beef.

EGGPLANT

Fruit of the *solanum melongena*; containing small amount of incomplete protein and small quantity of carbohydrates; having a relatively small percentage of mineral elements and proportionately large alkali excess; vitamin content not exactly determined; apparently rich in vitamins A and B and, perhaps C.

Eggplant is of the same family as the tomato. They do not taste well when eaten raw, and must, therefore, be stewed or baked. They have very little taste and so should be supplemented by aromatic herbs or other vegetables. Eggplant is said to have a calming effect upon the nerves.

EGGS

Eggs of various kinds of birds, especially hen's eggs; very rich in protein, egg yolk and fat; rich in potassium, sodium and chlorine; particularly rich in phosphorus acid; having high acid excess and small quantity of vitamin B and some of vitamins A and D.

Eggs are greatly overestimated as a food, especially since they contain a great deal of water. In popular opinion soft-boiled eggs are considered very nourishing and quite easy to digest. In reality, however, hard-boiled eggs, if well chewed, are much less difficult to digest.

EGG, WHITE OF

Rich in valuable protein; also rich in potassium, sodium and sulphur acid and chlorine; having fairly strong acid excess and only small proportion of vitamin B.

The whites are the least nutritious part of the eggs. They are used in cooking, especially in baked foods as a mixing ingredient.

EGG, YOLK OF

Rich in valuable protein, fat and lecithin (a waxy crystallizable substance with a high phosphorus content) ; rich in potassium and sodium; proportionately rich in calcium and sulphur; containing an unusually large amount of phosphorus, partly derived from its lecithin content; having strong acid excess and small quantity of vitamin B; very rich in vitamins A and D.

Because of their lecithin content egg yolks are recommended for nervous persons. Egg yolks are best when combined with fruit juices. Because of its high, fat-soluble vitamin content, an egg yolk added to a baby's milk will prevent rickets and strengthen the bones.

ENDIVE

Green and yellow leaf of the endive plant (*cichorium endivia*) of which there are many cultivated varieties; containing a small amount of inferior protein and small quantity of carbohydrates; rich in bitter ingredients; very rich in potassium and calcium; having strong alkali excess; rich in vitamin B (green varieties rich in vitamin A). Endives are especially good in salads. They are, however, very tough and must be thoroughly chewed. Because of their bitter ingredients they stimulate the appetite and the spleen (a gland-like organ on the left side of the body near the cardiac end of the stomach). Endives also promote the secretion of the bile and stimulate the activity of the skin.

FAT, COCOANUT

Extracted fat of the cocoanuts (*cocos nucifera*); containing practically no chemical except fat; having acid excess and hardly any traces of the vitamins.

Of all fats, cocoanut fat is the easiest to digest. It is decidedly the best substitute for butter. The chief characteristic of cocoanut fat is that it never goes rancid or stale.

FENNEL

Leaves and stalks of the *foeniculum vulgare;* containing small amount of incomplete protein and small proportion of carbohydrates; having fairly large percentage of mineral elements; possessing alkali excess. Fennel is principally used as a condiment, or for flavoring salads and soups. It promotes digestion of foods in the stomach, helps to regulate menstruation, lessens the production of mother's milk and has a strong diuretic action. Tea made from fennel is useful in loosening the phlegm in catarrh.

FIG

Fruit of the fig tree (*ficus carica*); but some figs are derived from the fig cactus (*opuntia*); rather deficient in protein; very rich in sugar (when dried, proportionately rich in protein and having large amount of raw fiber); very rich in calcium, potassium, magnesium and phosphorus acid; containing high alkali excess; rich in vitamin B. Figs contain a beneficial, protein-decomposing ferment called *papain*. Fresh figs are most nutritious and luscious. As a rule figs are dried before shipping.

The best figs are soft and mealy in appearance. Otherwise, it would be safe to assume that they have been treated with sulphuric acid or glazed with sugar water. Either of these two methods detract from the natural food value of the figs.

Figs strongly stimulate the digestive organs and are one of the best natural purgatives. They are beneficial to bladder secretion and for liver diseases and are especially recommended for gout, kidney disorders and haemorrhages. Children should be given figs in preference to candy.

FILBERT: See HAZELNUT

FISH

Flesh of fish is much easier to digest than animal meat; in general very rich in light, easily decomposed, valuable protein; having greatly varying fat content; containing a small amount, if any, carbohydrates; when fresh from the sea, rich in potassium, sodium and phosphorus and sulphur acids; salt water fish are also rich in iodine; having strong acid excess.

Because fish are very rich in organic compounds of phosphorus they are considered an excellent brain and nerve food. However, it must not be forgotten that the cause of the degeneration of the brain and nerves is not a phosphorus deficiency in diet, but that improper diet has made it impossible for the weakened nerve tissues to assimilate the phosphorus element in food. In nerve diseases of this kind, however, a strict vegetarian diet is unquestionably the best.

CARP: Having tender delicious flesh, rich in fat, this fish is a species of the *cyprinus carpo* of which there are many varieties.

EEL: One of the most delicious of fish, but its flesh, especially when smoked, is considered hard to digest because of its rich fatty content.

HADDOCK: This fish is at its best immediately after catching. It begins to deteriorate one or two hours after and gives off a strong odor. Haddock is easily digested and has comparatively little fat.

HALIBUT: An especially delicious variety of fish, fairly rich in fat.

PERCH: (*Percha fluviatilis*) River perch. One of our most valuable fresh-water fish. Its flesh is firm, fairly fat and most delicious. Perch is commonly thought to be bony, but when properly dissected the edible part is found to contain very few bones. Large perch, compared with pike or pike-perch, are decidedly more appetising.

PIKE: Small pike, weighing up to two pounds, are noted for their delicious, but lean flesh and are most appetising when well prepared. The flesh of the larger pike is tough and stringy and has no particular taste. Pike is best when pickled or broiled. These fish, however, contain many bones.

SALMON: Different varieties of the salmon species; noted for their tender, pink flesh; fairly rich in fat and very delicious. California or Alaska canned salmon is over-heated during its preparation and, therefore, inferior. Smoked or pickled salmon is very hard to digest.

SOLE: One of the finest and daintiest of our salt fish. The flesh is tender, easily digested and delicious, but poor in fat ingredients.

TROUT: Salmon trout and other salmon varieties belonging to one of our most delicate fresh-water species of fish. Trout are fairly rich in fat.

FOWL

Many people do not consider poultry meat to be the same as animal meat. This, of course, is a mistake since meat is composed of muscle, tissue and fat and it makes no difference whether it comes from fowl or animals. Also a great distinction is usually made between the white and dark meat of fowl because the white is believed to be more easily digested than the dark. In general, however, this idea is not correct. Poultry meat contains the same ingredients as animal meat; rich in potassium and phosphorus and sulphur acids; having high acid excess. Because of its high percentage of protein poultry meat should only be eaten in small quantities together with vegetables, salads or fruits.

GARLIC

Whole plant of the *allium sativum;* containing some incomplete protein; a proportionately large amount of sugar and raw fiber and some mustard oil; very rich in potassium, calcium and phosphorus acid; having fairly large alkali excess and traces of iodine; possessing sufficient quantities of vitamins B and C and traces of A.

Garlic is best eaten raw. Its very strong odor can be lessened by combining it with other garden herbs such as parsley, leeks, mint, etc.

Garlic plays an important rôle in modern dietary reform, but, nevertheless, it has always been a well-known and often favorite food. It is a common fact that all strong tasting foods are usually believed to have curative powers. For instance, all sharp tasting foods are supposed to have blood-cleansing properties. In a sense this does apply to garlic, since it is proportionately rich in vitamins and very rich in alkalies.

Garlic strongly stimulates the appetite and acid secretion of the gastric juices and so prevents flatulency or gas formation. This vegetable also promotes peristaltic action or the movement of the bowels and so tends to cure inflammatory conditions of the intestines and also cramps. Garlic is frequently recommended for the eradication of intestinal parasites and recently has been prescribed by some doctors for cholera.

Besides this, garlic has a beneficial effect upon the mucous membranes, especially in the upper air passages of the lungs, nose and throat and is, therefore, prescribed for singers and speakers. It is furthermore said to be helpful in gout, inflammation of the trachea, asthma and even in pulmonary tuberculosis. Many physicians are said to have used it with good results in cases of pulmonary consumption. Because of its iodine content it is also useful in treating goitre. Because of its vitamin content and alkali excess it is also valuable in conditions resulting from wrong dieting, as well as in cases of high blood pressure, over quick pulse and artery calcination. Finally, garlic has a diuretic action and aids in destroying stones. Although its diuretic action has been proven, garlic juice because of its mustard oil content is very irritating to the kidneys.

GINGER

Dried roots of a perennial plant (*zingiber officinale*); having small amount of incomplete protein, some carbohydrates and large quantity of sharp ethereal oil; rich in mineral elements;

having alkali excess; vitamin content unknown.

Cooked ginger is sometimes candied and so made into a delicious confection. Otherwise the root is almost always used as a spice in seasoning. Ginger increases the appetite and aids digestion, regulates delayed menstruation and has a diuretic action. Ginger eaten in large quantities tends to irritate the urethra and so to stimulate the reproductive instincts.

GOOSE

Different varieties of the *anser* species; very rich in fat; also rich in potassium and phosphorus and sulphur acids; having strong acid excess and small amount of vitamins A and B.

Goose flesh is as a rule tough and indigestible, with the exception of the breast which is more tender. When stuffed with sour fruits and roasted, the flesh becomes much more tender and is not so indigestible.

GOOSEBERRY

Fruit of the *ribes grossularia;* deficient in incomplete protein; when ripe rich in starches; rich in sugar and fruit acids; having small amount of vitamin B and large percentage of vitamin C.

Gooseberries are usually picked while still unripe, and then stewed. This method has its drawbacks, however, since the nutritive value of the ripe fruits is greater than that of the cooked, and also because they are more flavorsome.

Gooseberries, especially when unripe, have a mild purgative action. The downy skins of these berries stimulate the action of the intestines and help to overcome constipation. Gooseberries are recommended in general for cases of blood clotting, particularly in the liver.

GRAPEFRUIT

Fruit of the *citrus decumana*, the *pampelmus*; poor in protein and carbohydrates; very rich in fruit acids and their salts, above all in citric acids; rich in potassium; having an alkali excess; rich in vitamins B and C.

The slightly sour taste of grapefruit serves as a natural stomach bitter which increases the flow of the digestive juices. Grapefruit served at the beginning of a meal whets the appetite and later helps to digest other foods. Grapefruit juice helps to prevent over-weight, and when taken the last thing at night, aids in inducing sound sleep. As a drink the first thing in the morning this juice helps to overcome constipation and also aids in allaying fever.

GRAPE

Fruit of the different varieties of the vine, *vitis* species; poor in protein, what there is being incomplete; rich in fruit acid salts; especially vinous acid; rich in sugar and potassium; having alkali excess; rich in vitamins B and C.

Grapes, in common with dates, are a major food in the tropics. They are wholesome and

easily digested and for these reasons are prescribed in almost all illnesses. The popular
grape cure, according to Labbé, has various beneficial results to recommend it. To begin with,
by increasing and normalizing the urine, it drains
the system, lessens the formation of uric acid
while increasing the excretion of uric acid from
the body and decreases the amount of acid in the
body. The *grape cure* assures better intestinal
elimination, but in sensitive persons it may cause
diarrhea to develop. Because it assures better
food assimilation this diet tends to increase the
weight of the under-nourished. *Grape cures* are
to be recommended for the following conditions:
loss of appetite, hyper-acidity, constipation,
stomach catarrh causing phlegm, chronic diarrhea; blood clotting in the liver and in other
parts of the body, haemorrhages, gallstones, in-
fectious jaundice, gout and rheumatism, uric acid
conditions, inflammation of the kidneys and the
bladder, even for uremia and also in cases of
inflammatory skin diseases such as eczema and
akina (a disease causing pimples); high blood
pressure, corpulency, lung bleeding and nervous
disorders.

Grape cures cover so wide a range that they
are even recommended in certain mental disturbances and in weakened conditions of the entire
muscular system, especially the heart. They are
also beneficial for women in confinement and for
infants. They are helpful in all over-acid conditions. In tuberculosis and gout, however,

caution must be used, because sometimes those who are suffering from these diseases are no longer able to assimilate the sugar properly and it is converted into acid.

GUAYAVAS

Fruit of the *psidium quajava* and *cattleianum;* containing small amount of incomplete protein and fairly large quantity of sugar and starches; mineral element content unknown; vitamin content also unknown.

HAM

Salted and smoked upper thigh of the domestic pig (*sus domesticus*); rich in protein and fat; also rich in potassium, sodium, chlorine and in phosphorus and sulphur acids; having large acid excess; containing no vitamins.

Owing to its method of curing with kitchen salt and by smoking, ham is more injurious than other kinds of meat. The constant and almost exclusive use of such foods as ham will undoubtedly cause illness.

HAWS, SCARLET

Fruits of the different *crataegus* varieties; containing small amount of incomplete protein and fairly large quantities of sugar and starches; mineral element content unknown; having alkali excess; vitamin content also unknown.

HAZELNUT

Nut of the different *corylus* varieties; the filbert nut, an Italian variety of the *corylus avel-*

lana being considered the best; rich in complete and fairly valuable protein; containing small quantity of carbohydrates; rich in potassium, calcium and phosphorus and sulphur acids; having small acid excess and fair proportion of vitamin B and traces of vitamins A and C.

Hazelnuts or filberts are an excellent protein-supplying food, and for this reason and because of their acid excess should be eaten only in moderation. These nuts are firm in texture and consequently very indigestible, unless thoroughly chewed. Those who have poor teeth should eat hazelnuts only after they have been crushed, and for those with weak digestive organs these nuts should be finely ground. At one time they were recommended for those who had kidney stones as they were said to loosen and soften these abnormal formations. Hazelnuts should always be eaten together with fruits.

HERRING

Culpea harengus, species of fish; rich in protein and fat; rich in potassium, sodium and phosphorus and sulphur acids; showing traces of iodine; having large alkali excess; rich in vitamins A, B and D. The last vitamin is found mostly in the liver of the fish.

From the taste standpoint herring is very much underrated. Epicures declare that if herring was as scarce as salmon it would cost twice as much as that favorite, pink-fleshed fish. There are many delicious ways of preparing this fish. It is a most popular food from both the taste and price standpoint. It should, however, always be remembered that herrings are especially rich in protein and acid and should be eaten with plenty of vegetables.

HERRING, SALTED

Common herring salted; Matjes herrings, or young, undeveloped herrings are very fat, having same composition as the unsalted variety; rich in vitamins A and D, not in B. Salted herrings are very popular. They constitute an excellent protein-supplying food, but precisely on this account and also because of their high salt content, salted herrings should be eaten with caution.

HICKORYNUT

Ripe fruit of the *carya porcina* and *tomentosa*; rich in protein, fat and starch; also rich in phosphorus and sulphur acids and chlorine; rich in potassium; fairly rich in iodine; having acid excess and some vitamin B with traces of vitamin A.

Hickorynuts are very beneficial because of their valuable protein, especially for children. They must, however, be eaten only in small quantities and then combined with plenty of fruits.

HONEY

Nectar of flowers transformed into honey through digestion in the ante-stomachs of honey bees or the workers in the hive; composed almost entirely of grape and fruit sugar with a trace of formic acid; poor in mineral elements; having small acid excess and no vitamins; containing various animal ferments, most especially oxydase (oxydizing ferment).

Honey is useful in loosening phlegm and has a slight purgative action. It possesses a decided diuretic effect which does not in any way harm the kidneys. Strange to say, fresh honey that has never been heated is relatively easy for diabetic patients to digest. Honey is also thought to contain a heart hormone.

HONEY, ARTIFICIAL

Made from a mixture of starches combined with the acid salts of grape sugar, which is all artificially imbued with honey perfume; containing hardly any mineral elements and absolutely no vitamins nor enzymes.

Artificial honey is an inferior substitute for natural honey, but there is little need for it since real honey is so plentiful. Artificial honey lacks the curative properties of the natural honey.

HORSE RADISH
See RADISHES.

HUCKLEBERRY

Ripe fruit of the *myrtillus niger;* very poor in protein; fairly rich in sugar; very rich in fruit and tannic acids; containing fair amount of potassium; having alkali excess; possessing large quantity of vitamin B and some vitamin C.

Huckleberries are chiefly known for their tannic acid content. They have an astringent, anti-fermenting and binding action; therefore, they are recommended in cases of diarrhea, dysentery and intestinal bleeding.

Crushed huckleberries may be used externally applied to wounds and festering sores. The leaves of the huckleberry bushes contain an insulin-like ingredient, and an extract made from them is recommended for diabetes. In reality, however, we could detect no improvement in diabetic patients after this treatment. This is easily explained by the fact that the insulin ingredient is destroyed during the digestive process.

JUNIPER BERRY

Ripe, blue black berry of the common juniper tree (*juniperus communis*); fairly rich in inferior protein; rich in sugar, tannin and ethereal oils; rich in potassium, magnesium and phosphorus acid; having traces of fluorine and alkali excess; rich in vitamins B and C.

Juniper berries are eaten in various parts of the world, either raw or cooked, and they are also fairly popular as a condiment. They have a diuretic action. As a matter of curiosity it is interesting to know that a constant and continued consumption of juniper berries, owing to the oxidizing process of the turpentine and ethereal oil content in the system, causes the entire body and especially the urine to give off a distinct perfume similar to that of violets.

KALE

Leaves of the open cabbage varieties (*brassica oleracea* var. *acephala*) : containing small amount of incomplete protein and some carbohydrates; having plentiful supply of potassium and some calcium; possessing alkali excess; rich in vitamins B and C.

Kale is eaten like white cabbage or Savoy cabbage. It is excellent in all excess-acid conditions, but is somewhat likely to cause gas.

KALE, SEA

Sprout and young leaf of the sea kale (*cramba maritima*) ; containing some complete protein and small amount of sugar; rich in potassium and sodium; having some iodine; possessing alkali excess; vitamin content unknown.

Sea kale has been known for a long time and used by the ancients. Because of its iodine content it is recommended for goitre.

KALE, STALKS OF

Swollen stalks, grown above ground, of a cabbage variety (*brassica oleracea gongylodes*) ; a derivation of the common cabbage plant; containing large amount of incomplete protein; when young has a large quantity of sugar and small percentage of cellulose; when older becoming more woody; rich in potassium and calcium; possessing smaller quantities of sodium and magnesium and fair amount of phosphorus acid; having alkali excess; rich in vitamins B and C with traces of vitamin A. Kale can be eaten raw or it may be stewed, fried or baked.

LAMB

Meat of young sheep (lambs); rich in protein; containing some fat and large quantity of gluten; rich in potassium, sodium and phosphorus and sulphur acids; having strong acid excess and small amount of vitamin B. Lamb is a mild tasting meat, but nevertheless it is very popular. Like all meat, because of its high protein and acid content, it should be eaten with vegetables.

LAMB'S QUARTERS

Leaves and stalks of the ordinary *melde chenopodium album* and the more rare *chenopodium amaranthicolor* or Algerian variety; containing proportionately large amount of valuable protein and moderately large quantity of carbohydrates; having a large amount of mineral elements; possessing alkali excess; vitamin content unknown.

Lamb's quarters are still used as a spinach substitute in Northern countries where it grows wild. These leaves have a milder flavor than spinach, but they are said to contain the same food properties as those of the better known greens.

LARD

Melted fat extracted from the waste parts of the pig after it is slaughtered; consisting almost exclusively of fat; containing very few mineral elements of which the principal one is sulphur; having an acid excess and hardly any traces of vitamins.

Lard is an easily digestible fat; varying considerably in taste according to the feeding of the pig. Vegetable fats are superior to lard.

LEEK

Bulb and leaf of the *allium cepa*; containing small amount of protein, fair quantity of carbohydrates and small percentage of mustard oil; rich in potassium, sodium and phosphorus acid; having fairly strong alkali excess; rich in vitamins B and C.

Leeks are noted for their power in promoting urine secretion and in preventing flatulency. They are also recommended for inflammation of the air passages and for colds because they tend to loosen phlegm and to cure a cough. They also stimulate the action of the salivary and digestive glands and increase the appetite. Leeks are beneficial in treating gout, rheumatism, gallstones and heart pains. Ordinarily they are used only to flavor salads or as a condiment in preparing vegetables. This is a mistake since the leek in itself is an excellent vegetable which may be eaten either steamed or boiled.

LEMON

Fruit of the *citrus limonum* of which tree there are many varieties; containing small amount of incomplete protein; very rich in citric acid and citric acid salts; when ripe, rich in sugar; fruits, rich in potassium and calcium; having high alkali excess; fairly rich in vitamin B; very rich in C; lemon peel, very rich in ethereal oils; white of peel containing substantial quantity of vitamin A.

Lemons are usually shipped when still green. They should be used as a substitute for vinegar, and in making lemonade, a most refreshing beverage. Of all foods lemons are most universally known as a remedy. For more than four hundred years they have been used as a preventative and cure for scurvy. In the year 1700 the seamen in the British Navy were required to carry lemons and to eat them every day. Lemons counteract fever and are excellent, especially in the form of lemonade, for rheumatism. They have a diuretic action without injury to the kidneys, and therefore are successfully used in dropsy cases. Lemons are also helpful in treating heart pains and kidney inflammations. Because of their excess alkali content lemons have a strong action in curing an abnormal, glutinous condition of the blood and are, therefore, used as an internal and external remedy for inflammation of the lymphatic glands and also for varicose and ulcerated veins. Lemons help to relieve burning of the fingers and toes and are recommended in cases of high blood pressure. Lemons are beneficial in all types of blood disorders and also, because of their laxative effect, in curing colds.

In Southern Europe, where the people are of an emotional temperament, it is said that lemons, when eaten frequently, will calm the passions. Lemons are often used in reducing diets. Used externally, lemon juice is exhilarating and refreshing to the skin and helps to cure inflammation and festering sores. On that account it is especially recommended for mouth sores (abscesses or ulcers), swollen gums, sore throat and tonsilitis. Lemon juice also has healing properties for chilblains and chapped skin.

LENTIL

Ripe fruit of a papilionaceous plant (having butterfly-like flowers) *lens esculenta;* very rich in inferior protein and carbohydrates; also rich in cellulose; containing large quantity of purine; very rich in potassium, sodium and calcium; over rich in phosphorus and sulphur acids; having high acid excess and traces of vitamin B and small amount of vitamin A.

Because of their abundance of protein, lentils have been greatly overrated. Their protein content is incomplete and, therefore, requires the addition of other proteins. Lentils are hard to digest and a good percentage of them are carried through the digestive tract in an undigested state. They will cause gas unless they are eaten with vegetables and fruits.

LETTUCE, HEAD OF

Open or closed head leaves of the *lactuca sativa* in its different varieties; poor in organic food elements; containing some caoutchouc (rubber), chyle and also bitter ingredients; rich in potassium and calcium; possessing fairly large quantity of sodium; rich in iron; having some iodine; also strong alkali excess; containing sufficient of vitamins A, B and D and large quantity of vitamin C.

Heads of lettuce are very refreshing and healthful. Whenever salads are mentioned, one invariably thinks of lettuce. It has been discovered that the darker green, outer leaves contain most of the vital food elements. These leaves, therefore, should be finely chopped and sprinkled over the lettuce hearts when lettuce is served alone or in salads. Because of its abundance of vitamins and pronounced alkali excess, it is a potent remedy for all metabolic diseases. In fact, there is hardly any illness in which green salads can not be beneficially given. Even in cases of stomach ulcers, raw salads can be taken provided that the lettuce is very finely ground or chopped. When eaten in large quantities, lettuce is especially helpful in gout, tuberculosis and goitre. Lettuce juice is also recommended as an addition to bottled milk when babies must be artificially fed.

Lettuce heads stimulate the salivary glands and the appetite. Although not sufficiently recognized as yet, the pickled stalks or mid-ribs of sprouting lettuce leaves before blooming (after blooming they have a bitter taste) make an exceedingly delicious vegetable dish which might be compared to asparagus. Lettuce has a strong diuretic action which does not harm the kidneys and so is particularly beneficial in cases of dropsy.

LETTUCE, LAMB'S

Young, unblossomed plant of the *valerianella olitoria*; comparatively rich in protein; containing small amount of carbohydrates; unusually rich in sodium; having slight alkali excess; rich in vitamins B and C; possessing some of vitamins A and D.

Lamb's lettuce is a delicious salad plant, preferred by many to ordinary lettuce. It is, however, somewhat firmer in texture and, therefore, requires more thorough mastication. Lamb's lettuce is especially in demand since it begins to grow under the snow in early spring, and furnishes the first salad of the year. This plant was an Old World remedy for scurvy and also rightly renowned as a blood cleansing and refreshing agent.

LETTUCE, SEA

Leaves of the *cramba maritima*; containing few organic food elements; having large quantities of potassium, calcium and iodine; (it is

the richest in iodine of any cultivated plant).
Rich in vitamins B and C; possessing small
quantities of vitamins A and D.

Because of its high iodine content sea lettuce
is the best remedy for goitre.

LIME

Fruit of the *citrus limetta*, produced by cross-
ing lemons and oranges; also called "sweet
lemons"; containing small quantity of incomplete protein; fairly rich in sugar; very rich in
citric acid and citric acid salts; rich in potassium and calcium; having alkali excess and
fairly large amount of vitamin B; very rich in
vitamin C.

Limes are often used in place of lemons, and
in their ripe state, in place of oranges. They
are an excellent remedy for over-acid conditions
such as rheumatism and arthritis.

LIVER

Liver of various animals that feed their young
with their own milk, especially the cow and pig;
sheep's liver being less valuable because of its
strong taste; very rich in valuable protein, but
also in glandular protein and consequently in
uric-acid-forming ingredients; rich in potassium,
sodium and magnesium; very rich in phosphorus
aud sulphur acids; having large acid excess; containing small amount of vitamin B, large quantity of vitamin A, and in the livers of pasture-fed
animals also vitamin D.

Liver is supposed to be very indigestible and because of its rich protein, uric acid and excessive acid contents should only be eaten in small quantities. Recently, scraped raw liver has been widely used as a specific remedy for a real blood deficiency or pernicious anemia. Now the beneficial substance has been taken from the liver and put on the market so that these unfortunate sufferers no longer have to consume repugnant raw liver.

LOBSTER

Various marine varieties of the *astacus* species; rich in valuable protein; containing small amount of fat; very rich in potassium. sodium and phosphorus and sulphur acids; possessing traces of iodine; having large acid excess and small amounts of vitamins A and B.

Lobsters are held in high esteem, but due to their high protein and excess acid contents they should never be eaten in great quantities.

There flesh is tougher and their flavor decidedly inferior to that of crab meat. Lobsters are frequently recommended to nervous people as a brain and nerve food.

MACARONI

Meal or wheat-grits made from dough mixed with water to which eggs are sometimes added, which is afterwards formed into pipe or ribbon formations and dried in a low temperature. Genuine or pure macaroni also undergoes a ripening process by which the wheat protein (similar to the cheese protein in cheese ripening) is altered; containing fair amount of incomplete protein, small proportion of fat and large quantity of starches; rich in potassium and phosphorus and sulphur acids; having acid excess and small amount of vitamin B.

Macaroni is a highly concentrated food which, due to its surplus acid content, should only be eaten with vegetables and fruits. Macaroni and meat make a very poor food combination.

MALT

Germinated seeds of different grain varieties, usually barley (*hordeum vulgare*); the life in the seed being killed by a heating process; containing incomplete protein and small amounts of fat and starches; having large quantity of malt-sugar; rich in potassium and phosphorus and sulphur acids; possessing strong acid excess and fair amount of vitamin B.

Through the germination of the seeds a starch-transforming enzyme called diastase is developed which converts starches into sugar. Malt is not a popular food product and is principally used in the making of bread. On the other hand, a great importance is attached to the watery, evaporated extract made from malt. This extract is composed principally of malt-sugar or Maltose, and it is fairly rich in vitamin B. Malt extract is very popular as a strengthening tonic. It is most refreshing when taken after great physical exertion, which is also true of sugar or honey.

MANDARIN

Fruit of the *citrus nobilis* and *citrus deliciosa* which come from Lower Asia; containing small amount of protein, large quantity of sugar and free and combined fruit acids, especially citric acid; rich in potassium and calcium; having large alkali excess; containing sufficient vitamin B and a very large quantity of vitamin C.

Mandarins contain almost as much citric acid as lemons, but, nevertheless, are much sweeter. Their odor is peculiar and repellent to many. These fruits are a well-known remedy for intestinal sluggishness and constipation as well as for diseases caused by an over-acid condition. They are also a specific cure for scurvy and are easily digested by those suffering from diabetes.

MANGO

Fruit of the *mangifera indica*, originally an East Indian tree; containing very small amount of incomplete protein, fairly large quantity of sugar and small percentage of mineral elements; having small alkali excess; vitamin content unknown.

Mangos are extraordinarily popular in India. Mangos are credited with blood-cleansing and fever-soothing properties. They are also said to induce perspiration.

MAPLE SYRUP

Sap of the maple tree (*acer saccharinum*) native of North America, sap containing about 5 to 6 per cent of sugar. Usually the sap is brought to syrup thickness by evaporation; the resultant syrup containing a large quantity of sugar; rich in potassium and calcium; having alkali excess; in raw state, rich in vitamin B; after evaporation, having less vitamin B. Maple syrup was formerly prepared by simply evaporizing the sap over an open fire. Now it is evaporated in vacuum in the same manner as sugar juice. The sugar is saved by this new process, but its natural, pleasant taste is lost.

MARGARINE

Fat of the same consistency as butter, obtained by squeezing out the most easily melted ingredients of animal and vegetable fats, which by churning with skimmed milk, or better with cream, and by adding an artificial yellow coloring acquires the taste and appearance of butter; having in general very small proportions of mineral elements; containing acid excess; animal margarine having traces of vitamin A; vegetable margarine, none.

A great prejudice against margarine exists which is, however, unjustified. Margarine is a good fatty food and is easy to digest even when it is made from hardened oil. Others consider margarine of little value because it is not rich in vitamin A. This is a mistake since margarine is a fat-supplying food and as such is useful. Vegetables and fruits may be depended upon to furnish the body with vitamins.

MATÉ

Dried or fumigated leaves of the *ilex paraguayensis,* a South American plant; poor in protein, fat and carbohydrates; containing some mattein; rich in potassium; having alkali excess and no vitamins.

Maté is often extolled because it is thought to be less harmful than Chinese tea. This is true in most cases, but there are varieties of maté which contain just as much caffeine as Chinese tea.

Dr. Moreau de Tours of the Pasteur Institute states that the alkaloid in Maté contains the different properties of caffeine without presenting any of the inconveniences.

Because of its excess alkali content Maté is especially recommended for gout, and when consumed in large quantities often proves a beneficial treatment.

MEAT EXTRACT

Liquids pressed out of raw beef. In present-day manufacture, however, the genuine meat juice is used in making bouillon seasoning. Then after the liquids have been pressed out of the meat it is afterwards washed in lye. This water extract is boiled down to a syrupy thickness, usually strongly salted, and then sold as meat extract; containing some albumose, all the amino acids and all the flesh ingredients of the meat; very rich in potassium, calcium and especially rich in magnesium; having large quantities of phosphorus and sulphur acids and kitchen salt; possessing high acid excess and no vitamins. Because of its meat ingredients, meat extract, almost more than any other foods strongly stimulates the appetite and digestion and also the nerves. It is most often used as a foundation for soups, but vegetable extracts are much to be preferred.

MELON

Ripe fruit of the *cucurbita melo;* having small amount of incomplete protein, fair quantity of sugar and large proportion of cellulose; rich in potassium; having alkali excess; rich in vitamin B; containing fair amount of vitamin C.

Melons are excellent fruits which are highly valued. They are recommended for dropsy since they have a diuretic action which does not injure the kidneys. Melons are easier to digest when lemon juice is sprinkled over them.

MILK

Milk of various animals who feed their young with milk, especially the cow and the goat; rich in valuable protein; having fair proportion of easily digestible fat and large quantity of sugar (*milk lactose*) ; rich in potassium, calcium and phosphorus and sulphur acids; having small alkali excess; rich in vitamins A and B and according to the season of the year and the fodder of the animals, containing some vitamins C or D; possessing oxidizing ferments.

Milk is a very valuable food which, however, is greatly overrated. It is generally represented as an ideal food. It is for the calf during its nursing period, but not for humans. For the baby, cow or goat milk contains too much protein and too little alkali. In boiling or sterilizing and even in the pasteurizing process milk undergoes various changes by which its nourishing qualities, especially for the young child, are considerably lessened. In short, the vitamin content is changed, the valuable protein is partially decomposed and the bone-building salts in colloidal-loose form are changed to a combined form which is not easily assimilable. Whenever possible, the very young baby, deprived of mother's milk, should always be given fresh, unheated milk or milk which has only been brought to the boiling point. Milk, used in feeding babies, should come from good farms where the cows are certain to be free from tuberculosis. It should be thinned with water so that the protein content is lowered, and for that reason also should be tempered with sugar lactose or cream in order to help the infant to gain strength. Furthermore, lemon, or even better, orange juice should be given after feedings, as well as spinach or carrot juice, so that the infant will receive the necessary vitamins and bone-building salts.

For a long time goat's milk was thought to be the best substitute for mother's milk, but this is a mistake. Goat's milk is too deficient in iron and for that reason babies, fed upon it, become anemic.

MILK, BUTTER

Slightly curdled milk from which the fat has been removed. Its composition is almost the same as sour milk with the exception that it is deficient in fat. Buttermilk is good for those who wish to reduce.

MILK, SKIMMED

Milk from which the fat has been taken by skimming or separating. Composition is much the same as ordinary milk except that it contains only traces of fat.

MILK, SOUR

Milk curdled as the result of the formation of lactic acid by the normal development of lactic acid bacteria; the casein being transformed into gelatinous masses. The composition of sour milk, except that it has a smaller amount of sugar, is the same as that of ordinary, sweet milk.

Sour milk is especially recommended for those who can not digest fresh milk, especially to those suffering from stomach or intestinal complaints. In treating diarrhea sour milk often proves very helpful.

MILLET

Ripe seeds of the various *sorghum* (cereal grass) varieties; containing large quantity of incomplete protein, small amount of fat and large proportion of starches; rich in potassium, magnesium and phosphorus and sulphur acids; having strong acid excess and small amount of vitamin B.

Millet is used to a large extent in the tropics in the place of other grains, and is ground into a coarse meal for the making of bread. It has no advantages over our common varieties of grains.

MIRABELLE

Yellow fruit of the *prunus insititia;* having incomplete protein content and large quantity of sugar; rich in fruit acids and fruit acid salts; especially rich in potassium; having alkali excess and small amount of vitamin A.

Mirabelles are a good food which can be beneficially used in all diseases.

MOLASSES

Uncrystallizable, evaporated syrup obtained from the raw cane sugar residue when reduced to a fluid state by boiling; consisting of a mixture of raffinose, sucrose, grape and fruit sugars, etc.; having no protein content; very rich in mineral elements, especially potassium; containing large alkali excess, but no vitamins.

Molasses serves as an excellent sweetening

product especially for children's milk, porridges
or cereals.

MORILS

Flowering fruit of the moril varieties, grown
above ground; rich in incomplete protein; rich
also in potassium and phosphorus and sulphur
acids; having acid excess; vitamin content unknown.

Morils contain the poisonous helvellic acid
and, therefore they should be scalded with boiling water so that they may be eaten without
harm. They are a very delicious fungus food,
but, nevertheless contain excessive acids.

MULBERRY

Ripe fruit of the white or black mulberry tree
(*morus alba* and *nigra*); containing small percentage of protein, apparently incomplete, and a
fair amount of sugar; rich in potassium; having
alkali excess; fairly rich in vitamin B and containing small amount of vitamin C. The black
mulberries are sweeter and more flavorsome than
the white. In olden times mulberries were very
popular, and were considered as a general cure-
all. They are thirst quenching and helpful in
relieving inflammation of the mouth and tongue
as well as in treating chronic constipation.

MUSHROOM

Flowering fruit of the *agaricus campester* and
pratensis, grown above ground; fairly rich in

incomplete protein; containing some carbohydrates; rich in potassium, sodium and sulphur; having small alkali excess; possessing some vitamin B and a few traces of vitamin A.

Mushrooms are considered the leading fungus food, and make an excellent substitute for meat.

MUSKMELON

Fruit of the *cucurbita moschata;* containing small amount of incomplete protein and a fair quantity of sugar; rich in potassium; having an alkali excess and a moderate proportion of vitamin B. Muskmelons have a strong diuretic action without injuring the kidneys.

MUSSEL

Soft part of sea mussels *(myrtilus edulis)*; rich in valuable protein and fat; containing large amounts of sodium and calcium, large quantities of phosphorus and sulphur acids and some iodine; having an acid excess; rich in vitamin B; possessing some of vitamins A, D and C.

Mussels are a valuable protein food, which, however, on this very account should be eaten only in small quantities. Mussels, like fish, are often considered as a nerve food because of their richness in phosphorus acid. This, however, is mere superstition, unfounded by fact. It is important to make sure when eating raw mussels that they come from the fresh, open sea; otherwise they may contain disease-carrying bacteria. They must, furthermore be living when opened as the flesh quickly putrefies and can then cause fatal flesh poisonings. If the shells of the mussels are open, they are dead and unfit for food. The shells must always be firmly closed.

MUSTARD GREEN

Leaf and young stalk of the *sinapis arvensis;* containing moderate amount of valuable protein, small quantity of carbohydrates and fairly large percentage of mineral elements; having an alkali excess; vitamin content unknown.

Mustard greens can be eaten raw or stewed in their own juice or used as a spinach substitute. They are an excellent, savory vegetable which was at one time extensively cultivated. The ripe seeds of mustard greens contain mustard which is very strong and also a very irritating ethereal oil. These seeds, on the other hand, are very rich in fat and were formerly used as a lubricating food.

MUTTON

Flesh of the fully grown sheep (*ovis caprea*); rich in valuable protein; partially rich in fat; rich in potassium and phosphorus and sulphur acids; containing high acid excess and small amount of vitamin B with traces of vitamin A.

Mutton is a valuable protein food which, however, due to its pronounced taste is not enjoyed by everyone. Because of its rich protein content and its excessive acids, mutton should be eaten in small quantities and then always with vegetables. Mutton fat is very difficult to digest.

NECTARINE

Ripe fruit of a peach variety (*prunus persica nectarina*); fairly rich in carbohydrates, particularly in sugar; containing small amount of minerals, especially potassium; having some alkali excess; vitamin content unknown.

Nectarines are very refreshing and flavorsome fruits.

NETTLE

Leaf of the *urtica urens* and *dioica;* fairly rich in incomplete protein and carbohydrates; very rich in potassium and calcium; having an alkali excess; rich in vitamins A, B and C with traces of D; containing a hormone similar to the secretion which stimulates digestion.

Because the leaves are covered with prickly hairs, nettles must be ground or chopped before they can be appetizing. In flavor, however, they are superior to spinach and are also more valuable as a food remedy than the more popular greens. Nettles can be eaten raw, stewed or steamed. They are a most effective remedy for all over-acid conditions and nearly all internal diseases. Raw nettle juice has a stimulating effect upon the secretion of the digestive glands.

NUTS

All genuine nuts are rich in protein, fat and carbohydrates; also in potassium, sodium, calcium and phosphorus and sulphur acids; having a small acid excess.

Many seeds are incorrectly referred to as nuts. They can be distinguished from the genuine nuts by the fact that they contain incomplete protein and a much higher acid excess. Among these so-called nuts are peanuts. Genuine nuts contain valuable protein and so should be eaten in combination with fruits.

OATS, ROLLED

Seed grains of the *avena sativa* crushed and husked by a rolling process; proportionately rich in inferior protein; very rich in starches; containing, depending upon the extraction, more or less fat; rich in potassium and phosphorus and sulphur acids and silicious acids; having acid excess and small amount of vitamin B with traces of vitamin A.

There are two kinds of rolled oats; those that have their seed jackets (not to be confused with husks) removed and those that have not. Those without their seed jackets are very inferior to the others which still contain within themselves all the nutritive elements of the grain. In North America the inferior variety is most frequently found.

Rolled oats from which the seed jackets have not been removed have the reputation for being most nutritious, but one must not forget that the protein is incomplete and that they contain excess acid.

Rolled oats are especially recommended for children, but they should be eaten with fruit. They can be eaten raw or cooked. If cooked, the best way to prepare them is to heat the water to a boiling point, gradually stir the oats into the hot water and cook for another two minutes.

OATS, STEEL-CUT

Broken seed grains of the *avena sativa* made by passing the grains through steel cutting machines. While steel-cut oats are very often derived from the jacketless seeds, meal is almost exclusively obtained from seeds with their jackets still unremoved. Steel-cut oats are fairly hard to digest and so are rather unsuitable for a raw food diet. These oats take longer to cook. All oat preparations are generally credited with having an insulin-like ingredient and are therefore recommended for diabetes. Falsely so, however, since the insulin is destroyed in the process of digestion. In reality, fruit rather than oat diets are to be preferred in the majority of diabetic cases.

OCA

Bulbs of the *oxalis tuberosa;* containing incomplete protein and moderate amount of starches; having alkali excess; vitamin content unknown. Oca is now and then cultivated and used as a potato substitute.

OKRA

Unripe seed pods of the *abelmoschus esculentus;* fairly rich in protein and carbohydrates;

rich in sodium and calcium; having alkali excess
and small amount of vitamin B.

Okra may be used as a condiment or eaten as a
vegetable and has a particularly strong taste.
Okra is recommended to those who wish to reduce; and in treatment of gall-bladder stones and
kidney stones.   It is also most beneficial in cases
of inflammation of the stomach or intestines.

OLIVE

Fruit of the olive tree (*olea europaea*); having
a small amount of incomplete protein and small
percentage of carbohydrates; very rich in fat
also rich in potassium, sodium and calcium; having a large alkali excess and a small amount of
vitamin B with traces of vitamin A.

Unripe olives, before they are ready to eat,
must be treated with lye in order to remove their
sharp and bitter taste.   They are still green when
shipped and are usually preserved in salt water.
Aside from their fat content they have no great
value as a food.   The ripe black olives should
also be preserved in salt water or they may be
dried and kept in olive oil.   The ripe black olives
are much richer in food elements of all kinds
than the unripe green fruit, and are much to be
preferred.   Olives, because of their oil content,
are said to act favorably upon the liver, to prevent gallstones and to relieve constipation.   The
ripe olives are also to be recommended for diabetes.

OLIVE OIL

This oil is the best and most healthful of all vegetable oils and is secured by means of the cold-press process from ripe olives. First-press oil is of a yellowish-green colour, and contains all of the goodness of the sun-ripened olives. Unfortunately, many of the olive oils on the market are of the second or third press, and may even be diluted with the cheaper vegetable oils, and therefore do not contain many of the healthful properties which the virgin olive oil of the first pressing contains. Olive oil is a valuable ingredient which should always be included in the making of salad dressing and mayonnaise. For a sluggish gall bladder or liver, olive oil with a bit of lemon taken upon rising in the morning acts as a lubricant, and helps to eliminate gallstones. First-press olive oil is much to be preferred to cod-liver oil.

ONION

Bulb of the different onion varieties (*allium*); having a small amount of incomplete protein and a fair percentage of sugar; very rich in ethereal mustard oil; rich in potassium and calcium; containing a large quantity of sulphur (from the mustard oil; having alkali excess which increases in proportion when the mustard oil content is smaller); possessing sufficient amount of vitamins B and C.

There are several inferior varieties of onion;

for instance the white pearl onion, the middle-sized purple onion and the middle-sized pale red onion, all of which are very rich in mustard oil. On the other hand, the full size, cultivated varieties, especially the Portuguese Giant onion, are very poor in mustard oil and rich in sugar. The former varieties are principally used as a condiment, while the latter are a valuable food.

Onions, in common with all sharp tasting foods, occupy an important place among popular "food remedies." They are recommended for colds, hoarseness, coughs, catarrh, dizziness (vertigo), dropsy, dysuria, loss of appetite, body and breast pains, flatulency, constipation, face aches, headaches, murmurings in the ears, worms, etc. They are regarded as a sort of general cure-all. In reality they are strongly diuretic in their action.

ORANGE

Ripe fruit of the different varieties of the *citrus aurantiacus;* having a small amount of incomplete protein and a fair quantity of sugar; very rich in citric acids and fruit acid salts; rich in potassium and calcium; having a large alkali excess; rich in vitamin B; very rich in vitamin A; possessing large amount of vitamin C, contained in the white inner covering of the orange peel.

Oranges are appropriately called "concentrated sunshine" when their curative powers are taken into account, even though their nutritive value is not particularly great.

We have already mentioned in our reference to lemons that they are the most widely used as a remedy of all foods. This is due to the greater ease with which the very sour lemons may be transported. Oranges, generally speaking, only became popular as a food within the last ten years. As a fact, oranges are far superior to lemons. Oranges are excellent for all conditions arising from incorrect diet, most especially in over-acid conditions. They are also beneficial for chronic sluggishness of the intestines. To overcome constipation they should be eaten early in the morning on an empty stomach, and again in the afternoon. Oranges may be considered as a specific remedy in cases of typhus, cholera, dysentery and ordinary diarrhea, as well as for intestinal catarrh of all kinds, even for tubercular catarrh. The treatment is to take three to twelve oranges daily without any other kind of food. Oranges are a necessity to children, and as long as they can be procured they should never be missing from the diet of adults.

The composition of oranges, especially in regard to their mineral elements, varies largely according to the different methods used in cultivation. This, however, only effects the quantity of their mineral ingredients, and has no special significance.

People who suffer from too much acid should

eat oranges after meals. In cases where there is a deficiency of stomach acids, the procedure should be reversed and the meals should begin with oranges.

OYSTER

Various oyster species, especially the *edulis;* fairly rich in valuable protein and containing some fat; rich in potassium, sodium and chlorine; also rich in phosphorus and sulphur acids; proportionately rich in iodine; having an acid excess; containing vitamin B and a small amount of vitamin A.

Oysters are most highly regarded as a food because of their valuable protein content which is very easily digested. For this reason they are especially recommended for people with weak digestive organs; although in reality the digestive organs are still further weakened by the very ease with which oysters are assimilated. Oysters should be eaten only in small quantities as is the case with all animal foods.

PALMETTO

Sprout and shoot of the *inodes palmetto;* containing moderate amount of inferior protein and small proportion of carbohydrates; having moderate percentage of mineral elements and apparently small acid excess; vitamin content unknown.

PAPAYA

Fresh fruit of the *carica papaya;* fairly rich in incomplete protein; rich in sugar and fat; also rich in sodium and magnesium; fairly rich in phosphorus and sulphur; having alkali excess; rich in papain, a protein digestant ferment; vitamin content unknown.

The white, pulpy flesh of the papaya, which somewhat resembles butter in its appearance, is eaten to a great extent, but principally in the tropics. It greatly stimulates the appetite and is a valuable aid to digestion. It is also particularly beneficial to those who suffer from too little secretion of juices in the stomach.

PAPRIKA

Ripe fruit of the *paprika* plant. Its skin is very rich in sharp-tasting ingredients which greatly irritate the mucous membranes. Paprika, therefore, should be eaten only in small quantities. It is said that paprika, like all strong tasting vegetables, acts as a blood cleanser, because it is assumed that the acrid ingredient "drives the acid out of the blood." This belief is not founded upon fact.

PARSLEY

Stalk and green leaves of the *petroselinum sativum;* having a small amount of fairly complete protein, also ethereal oil; rich in potassium, calcium and magnesium; possessing an alkali excess; containing a large amount of vitamins B and C and some of vitamin A. Parsley is one of the most valuable of the non-injurious, aromatic herbs and is usually employed as a flavoring or a garnish for food. When stewed in butter it can also be eaten as a vegetable and is most delicious.

Parsley, as is the case with all strong-tasting and odorous foods, is credited with great, blood-cleansing properties. Because of its ethereal oil content it is diuretic in its action. Parsley allays fever and is very effective as a remedy for dropsy provided that the kidneys have not been affected. It is also recommended in cases of menstrual irregularities and cramps. This herb stimulates the digestion and its healing properties are useful in urethra inflammation, liver and bile disorders and spleen diseases.

Parsley roots make a very delicious vegetable although disliked by some people because of their strong taste.

Parsley juice is also widely used as a popular remedy and is especially recommended for kidney and kidney stone complaints.

PARSNIP

Root of the *pastinaca sativa;* having a small amount of incomplete protein; fairly rich in sugar; very rich in cellulose; containing high amount of ethereal oil; rich in potassium and calcium; having an alkali excess and small amounts of vitamins A and B. Parsnips are put to the same use as carrots and far surpass the latter in the richness of their food values. They are strongly diuretic in their action and are recommended for gout, stone complaints and tuberculosis.

Parsnips, like all other strong-tasting foods, were formerly very highly rated by medical science; even being said to help in certain mental disorders.

The leaves of the cultivated variety of the parsnip, like those of the carrot, may be eaten as a vegetable and are delicious in flavor. The leaves of the wild parsnips contain a poisonous ingredient which acts in the same way as hemlock, although the poison seems to show itself more or less strongly in different parts of the body.

PEACH

Ripe fruit of the *prunus persicaria* of which there are many varieties; having a small amount of incomplete protein and a fair percentage of sugar; very rich in potassium; moderately rich in calcium; having an alkali excess; possessing sufficient quantities of vitamins B and C.

Peaches aid the digestion and the secretion of the digestive juices. They are both diuretic and laxative and, therefore, are most beneficial for dropsy. They are also recommended for bladder and kidney troubles.

The kernels, contained in peach stones, are rich in fat oil, but also contain some prussic acid.

PEANUT

Ripe seed (not nut) of a papilionaceous (having flower petals resembling butterflies) plant (*arachis hypagaea*) which in ripening bore their way into the ground; very rich in incomplete protein and in partly digestible fat; containing fair proportions of carbohydrates and purine; very rich in potassium, calcium, magnesium and phosphorus and sulphur acids; having strong acid excess; containing fair amount of vitamin B and small quantity of vitamin A.

The old idea that with washing peanuts acquire more uric acid and so become injurious is absurd. In reality, washed peanuts can be chewed more easily and are, therefore, more digestible. Peanuts are said to be an especially wholesome food, which is not entirely true, as in every respect they are inferior to the ordinary nut.

PEAR

Ripe fruit of the *pirus communis* of which there are many cultivated varieties; having a small amount of bad protein; fairly rich to very rich in sugar; moderately rich in potassium; having some alkali excess; containing small amount of vitamin B and still smaller amount of vitamin C. Pears, in common with apples, although in a lesser degree, have suffered from over-cultivation. They have been cultivated for so long with sole regard for their taste and appearance, that very much of their nutritive and curative powers have been lost. Pears are, nevertheless, valuable as a food, and are of great benefit in aiding digestion. The stone fiber or grit contained in the coarser varieties of pears are exceedingly irritating in cases of intestinal catarrh, especially in chronic cases. Pears have a fairly strong diuretic action and as their sugar content is principally composed of fruit sugar, they may be eaten, even when sweet, by diabetics without causing any harm.

PEA, FRESH

Unripe green seed and husk of the garden pea (*pisum sativum*) of which there are many cultivated varieties; fairly rich in incomplete protein, sugar and starches; rich in potassium, magnesium and phosphorus and sulphur acids; containing slight alkali excess and a fair amount of vitamins A, B and C.

Fresh green peas, still in growth, are entirely different from the completely ripe peas; since the ripe peas are really seeds while the fresh peas are considered as a vegetable. Fresh peas are very healthful when eaten raw and also nutritious when boiled or steamed. They have been cultivated for only a few centuries, nevertheless, there are a number of different varieties. The pods of the "sugar pod" varieties (like the pods of string beans) may be eaten as well as the unripe peas. When peas first became popular they were thought to possess every possible curative power. This belief, however, was founded only upon superstition. Peas have a slight diuretic action but otherwise no special healing properties.

PEA, DRIED

Ripe seed of the hard pea (*pisum sativum*) or field pea (*pisum arveuse*); rich in incomplete protein, fat and carbohydrates; very rich in potassium, calcium, magnesium and phosphorus and sulphur acids; having a decided acid excess and a fair amount of vitamins A and B.

Dried peas constitute a highly concentrated food, rather difficult to digest, and, therefore, should be eaten only in small quantities together with fruit.

PECAN NUT

A variety of the butter-nut. Very healthful and delicious. Pecans have the highest oil content of all nuts. They contain 71% of fat. Five medium-sized pecans represent as much energy food as two slices of bread or a cup of cooked oatmeal.

A finely ground meal or paste made of pecans is an easily digestible concentrated food, having a mild laxative effect due to the high oil content. Highly recommended as a building food.

PEPPER, BLACK

Unripe fruit of the pepper plant (*piper nigrum*); rich in sharp, acrid ingredients which irritate the mucous membranes, especially the kidneys and in an indirect way also the urethra and the reproductive organs. Black peppers were formerly recommended for malaria.

PEPPER, WHITE

Ripe, powdered fruit of the pepper plant (*piper nigrum*) which is often treated with lime; containing about twice as much acrid-tasting ingredients (*piperin*) as the black pepper. In spite of this, however, white pepper is milder because it contains less acrid resins. White pepper is forbidden to those afflicted with kidney complaints. It is wrongly recommended as a blood purifying remedy.

PERSIMMON

Ripe fruit of the persimmon; containing a small amount of incomplete protein and a fair quantity of carbohydrates; rich in potassium, magnesium and phosphorus acid; having a great alkali excess; vitamin content unknown.

Persimmons have a fairly strong purgative action. They are chiefly consumed in North America.

PICKLES

Small cucumbers and various other vegetables preserved in vinegar or strong mustard. Pickles should not be eaten regularly. They have no particular food value, being simply relishes to stimulate the appetite.

PIGWEED: See LAMB'S QUARTERS.

PINEAPPLE

Delicious fruit of the *ananassa sativa,* a plant which grows in tropical and sub-tropical countries; rich in potassium; having alkali excess; rich in malic, citric and tartaric acids; containing a high percentage of cellulose and a ferment known as papain, similar to pepsin in that it neutralizes protein acids.

Pineapples should be included in the family diet, not only because of their delightful flavor, but also because they are one of the best known remedies for poor digestion and constipation. They supply the weak stomach with the lacking acid salts and act as a disinfectant for the digesting food. Pineapple to some extent dissolves protein without the aid of acid salts and has a strong diuretic action. These fruits are of great benefit to women who are subject to retarded menstrual periods. They are also most helpful in curing nervous asthma.

PINE NUT

Ripe nut-like fruit of the different *pinus* varieties; rich in incomplete protein and fat; also rich in tannic acid; having strong acid excess and small amount of vitamin B.

Pine nuts have recently been highly recommended, however, erroneously so, as they can in no respect be compared to genuine nuts. The

protein content of pine nuts is incomplete. This
distinguishes them from genuine nuts.

PISTACHIO

Ripe fruit of the *pistacia vera*, a small tree,
native to Persia; very rich in protein, fat and
carbohydrates; having alkali excess; vitamin
content unknown.

Pistachios are supposed to increase the activity
of the reproductive organs and stimulate the
emotions.

PLUM

Fruit of the domestic plum (*prunus domestica*) in many different cultivated varieties, the
principal of which are the yellow plum (*prunus
insititia*) and the greengage; having some incomplete protein; very rich in sugar; containing a fair amount of fruit acid salts; rich in
potassium; possessing a moderate alkali excess
and a small quantity of vitamin B.

Plums are excellent fruits which are very helpful in all illnesses caused by an over-acid condition of the system. They are especially to be
recommended for rheumatism, gout, calcification
of the arteries and kidney inflammation; also for
constipation and hemorrhoids. Because of their
stimulating effect upon the intestines plums are
also recommended for liver complaints.

PLUM, DAMSON

Ripe fruit of the various *prunus* varieties;
poor in incomplete protein; when in ripe state,

rich in sugar; rich in potassium; having alkali excess and small amount of vitamin B.

Damson plums are a good fruit, best eaten raw. They are especially to be recommended for rheumatism, gout and degeneration and hardening of the arteries; also for inflammation of the kidneys. The fresh fruits have a strong diuretic action without injury to the kidneys. The dried damson plums or watery extracts derived from them have a strong purgative effect.

POKE BERRY SHOOT

Shoot of the *phytolacca americana;* having fairly large amount of inferior protein, mineral element content unknown; vitamin content unknown.

Poke berry shoots are eaten as a substitute for asparagus.

POMEGRANATE

Fruit of the *punica granatum,* native to Asia Minor; containing small quantity of incomplete protein and large amount of sugar; unusually rich in sodium; having alkali excess; rich in vitamins B and C.

Pomegranates are cut in two and eaten with a spoon, but one must be careful not to eat any of the skin or the partition walls of the fruits as these are rich in tannic acid and bitter ingredients and have a most unpleasant taste. The pulp of the fruits should be well chewed and the seeds taken from the mouth, not swallowed. Today, pomegranates are extensively used as a remedy in nearly all feverish conditions. The edible parts are slightly purgative while the skin and partition walls have a very constipating effect.

PORK

Flesh of the domestic pig (*sus domestica*); rich in protein and easily digestible fat; very rich in phosphorus and sulphur acids; having a high acid excess and hardly any traces of vitamins A and B.

Pork is a highly concentrated food which should be eaten seldom and then only in small quantities with plenty of vegetables and fruits.

PORTER

Strong, fermented beer brewed from germinated and thoroughly roasted barley to which sugar has been added; rich in carbohydrates and bitter tasting saccharin (not to be confused with the sweet ingredient saccharin); proportionately very rich in sodium; having small acid excess and hardly any traces of vitamins.

Formerly porter was principally used as a strengthening beverage; most often during convalescence, but wrongly so, since beverages containing alcohol never strengthen but merely stimulate the nerves.

POTATO

Underground bulb of the potato plant (*solanum tuberosum*); containing small amount of very valuable protein, large quantity of starches and traces of an alkaloid known as solanin; very rich in potassium; showing traces of iodine; possessing very strong alkali excess; having sufficient of vitamin B, a small amount of vitamin A and a large quantity of vitamin C.

The potato is one of the most valuable foods. The wild variety growing on the elevated plains of Central America has a sweet taste and is somewhat watery, but the common, cultivated variety has a firm texture and a delicious but indefinite taste. For this reason one never grows tired of potatoes and also because these vegetables can be prepared in so many different ways. The worst way to prepare potatoes, from the nutritive point of view, is to peel them raw and then boil them in salt water. This method destroys most of their curative powers and valuable food elements. The best way to cook potatoes is to bake them unpeeled in a hot oven. This way of cooking improves the taste. They may also be steamed or boiled in a little water with their jackets still on. When boiled without their jackets the water in which they were boiled and which contains many beneficial properties should be used with them as it improves the taste. This water also makes the best foundation for vegetable soups.

Potatoes are recommended for gout and sciatica. Diabetic patients frequently can digest potatoes better than bread, but there are also cases in which the reverse is true. Potatoes are especially good because of their vitamin C content, which is so great that even after the potatoes are cooked they still contain a sufficient amount of this vitamin to prevent scurvy. Remember that the valuable protein and the mineral elements are concentrated in the layer directly under the skin.

POTATO, SWEET

Root bulb of a Central American plant *convolvulus* or *ipomoea batatas* which is now also grown in the sub-tropical countries; containing a small amount of somewhat incomplete protein and large quantities of sugar and starches; very rich in potassium and calcium; having large alkali excess and traces of iodine; containing only small percentage of vitamin B and traces of vitamin C, but sufficient quantity of vitamin A.

Because of their great alkali excess sweet potatoes have certain medicinal powers. They are similar in some respects to white potatoes, although their vitamin content is not nearly so high. Sweet potatoes may be prepared in the same ways as white. The protein and mineral elements are concentrated in the layer immediately under the skin.

POTATO STARCH

Frequently used for thickening food products. It should be given preference over corn flour because it has a trace of alkali excess.

PRUNE

Dried fruit of the common plum; having small amount of incomplete protein; very rich in sugar and free cellulose; also rich in potassium and calcium; having high alkali excess and traces of vitamin B. Prunes are a very valuable food which may be given to children instead of candy. Because of their free cellulose content and their richness in fruit acids and fruit acid salts, prunes have a stimulating effect upon the digestion and help to overcome constipation. Cold prune juice taken before breakfast is especially effective for this purpose.

PUMPKIN

Fruit from different varieties of the *cucurbita* species; poor in protein; containing fairly large amount of sugar and a large quantity of free cellulose; rich in potassium and sodium; having small alkali excess; rich in vitamin B; containing some vitamin C.

They can be steamed, baked or lightly fried in a pan. Pumpkins are a delicious food and a good substitute for roasts. These vegetables, especially in their raw state, are very laxative. They have a strong diuretic action which does not irritate the kidneys and so are particularly to be recommended in all cases of dropsy. They are also effective in treating hemorrhoids. The unhusked seeds have a delightful almond-like flavor and are anthelminthic. (They destroy tapeworms and other parasitic worms in the digestive

tract.)   When preserving or pickling pumpkins
the seeds should always be included.

PURSLANE

Leaves and stalks of different varieties of the
portulaca; containing valuable protein and a
small amount of carbohydrates; having large
quantity of mineral elements; also high alkali excess; vitamin content unknown.

Purslane is principally used as a supplement
to green salad.   When stewed it can also be advantageously used as a spinach substitute or in
making soup.   This vegetable is said to have a
soothing effect upon irritations and inflammations of the mucous membranes.

QUINCE

Ripe fruit of the quince tree (*cydonia vulgaris*) ; rich in incomplete protein; fairly rich
in sugar; containing large quantities of fruit acid
and fruit acid salts and also tannic ingredients;
very rich in cellulose, stone cells and pectin
(jelly ingredient) ; rich in potassium; having an
alkali excess; vitamin content unknown.

In cold climates the quince seldom ripens and
is only edible when cooked.   In warm climates
the fruits become soft and sweet.   Because of
their tannic ingredient and pectin content these
fruits possess both laxative and binding properties.   Therefore, quince is recommended for intestinal weaknesses and disturbances of all kind.

Quinces are also used in tubercular cases and

in uterus or womb diseases. Due to their high protein content these fruits make an excellent jelly.

The Japanese quince (*cydonia japonica*) thrives only in warm climates, bears delicious, green fruits which make an exceptionally fine jelly. Quince is also renowned for its cooling properties and is, therefore, to be recommended in feverish illnesses.

RADISH

Sweet root bulb of the *raphanus sativus* of which there are two different varieties; the round, white, summer variety and the more elongated, red, winter variety; poor in incomplete protein; fairly rich in sugar; containing large quantity of mustard oil, especially in the skins of the red variety; having large amount of cellulose; rich in potassium; possessing alkali excess; vitamin content unknown.

Radishes contain a hormone similar to the secretion which stimulates the function of the stomach and intestines. Radishes are strongly diuretic. They also stimulate the appetite and digestion and are, therefore, valuable for stomach and intestinal complaints as well as liver and bile diseases. The mustard oil in radishes has a loosening effect upon catarrh, even in cases of a tubercular nature. This rich mustard oil content actually aggravates kidney diseases, nevertheless, because of its strong diuretic action radishes are sometimes recommended for this disease. It is best for sufferers from kidney complaints to refrain from eating radishes. The juice of raw radishes is prescribed to drive gallstones out of the bladder. This juice, mixed with sugar, helps to overcome catarrhal conditions.

RADISH, HORSE

Root of a perennial plant, *cochlearia armoracea;* containing small quantity of very inferior protein and hardly any traces of fat; having large amount of carbohydrates, much raw fiber and ethereal mustard oil; very rich in potassium, calcium and phosphorus acid; also very rich in sulphur acid; possessing some alkali excess; vitamin content unknown.

Horse radish would be a most beneficial food if it did not contain so much mustard oil. This oil, not only makes the taste much too strong, but also irritates the kidneys, the bladder and the mucous membranes of the digestive tract.

Horse radish is said to be a powerful diuretic remedy, formerly highly recommended in cases of dropsy. Nevertheless, these roots have an injurious effect upon the kidneys. They were also thought to be beneficial in treating skin diseases, hereditary weakness and colds. Horse radish stimulates the appetite and digestion and aids in loosening or dissolving phlegm.

The large leaves of the horse radish plant make a delicious green vegetable which deserves to be more popular than it is. Unlike the roots, the leaves have an alkali excess and contain hardly any mustard oil. They are also rich in vitamins A, B and C.

RAISIN

Dried fruit of the grape (*vitis vinifera*) ; small white varieties being known as sultanas; the small black kind being called currants; proportionately rich in inferior protein; very rich in sugar; fairly rich in free cellulose; rich in potassium, calcium, magnesium and phosphorus and sulphur acids and chlorine; having traces of iodine; possessing large alkali excess and small amount of vitamin B.

Raisins are a highly concentrated food. Their curative powers are practically the same as those of fresh grapes only one must remember that their vitamin content is much smaller. Raisins are a fine, nutritive food which can be easily carried by travelers and excursionists. When the heart, because of excessive exertion, beats feebly and irregularly, eat a handful of raisins and in twenty minutes the activity of the heart will once more be normal. A watery extract made from raisins, or better yet currants, is a popular remedy for catarrh and also diarrhea. For those who follow raw food diets raisins, owing to their rich alkali content, serve to balance the acid effect of oats and nuts.

RASPBERRY

Ripe fruit of the raspberry plant (*rubus idaeus*) ; ordinarily red, seldom yellow and still more seldom dark purple; containing small quantity of incomplete protein and fairly large amount of sugar; rich in protein; having fairly large alkali excess; possessing large quantity of vitamin C, and apparently also a large amount of vitamin B.

Raspberries are exceptionally flavorsome fruits, refreshing and stimulating. They are recommended for all illnesses resulting from an over-acid diet. Raspberry syrup is frequently given for inflammation of the air passages in order to loosen the phlegm.

RHUBARB

Leaves and stalks of the rhubarb varieties, especially the *rheum officinale* and *sibiricum;* containing very small quantity of protein, some sugar and large amount of fruit acid and salts, particularly oxalic acid; very rich in potassium; having alkali excess; concerning the vitamin content we can only detect the presence of vitamin C. Oxalic acid is a strong blood poison, two to five grams of which if administered to children would act fatally. One must, therefore, be extremely careful in eating rhubarb. Stewed rhubarb is best eaten with milk, since the lime in milk combines with the oxalic acid in rhubarb to form a harmless salt.

Rhubarb has a slightly laxative effect and is said to act favorably upon the lymphatic glands. It is not true, however, that rhubarb is of assistance in treating cancer. Rhubarb leaves, which are frequently recommended as a spinach substitute are much richer in oxalic acid than the rhubarb itself. In Central Europe during the War a great many fatal poisoning cases resulted from eating rhubarb leaves.

ROMAINE

Roman salad, a variety of the ordinary lettuce. Its composition is the same as that of common lettuce and it is excellent for all diseases due to too much acid in the system.

RUTABAGA

Underground root bulb of the *brassica napus esculenta;* containing small amount of incomplete protein, some carbohydrates, large proportion of cellulose and some mustard oil; having sufficient of vitamin B, large amount of C and small quantity of vitamin A.

Rutabagas can be prepared in many different ways; steamed, stewed or fried. These vegetables are recommended for chronic constipation, but, nevertheless, they cause a great deal of gas to form during digestion. Because of their mustard oil content they should not be eaten by those afflicted with kidney disorders.

SAUERKRAUT: See CABBAGE, WHITE, SOUR

SPINACH

One of the most popular of the leafy vegetables, spinach was originally brought to us from

Asia, where, even today, it grows wild. It contains complete and valuable protein, and is highly publicized as the most valuable vegetable for that reason. However, all of the dark green leafy vegetables contain the same healthful properties. Early spring spinach contains more of the valuable elements than the winter variety.

Spinach, as well as all other dark green leafy vegetables, is rich in mineral salts and vitamins, and to prevent their destruction spinach should be steamed in its own juice for not more than eight minutes. Raw spinach juice has a high content of alkaline forming elements, and iron; and also contains one of the newly discovered hormones which act favorably upon the glands.

SQUASH

Fruit of the different melon varieties, especially the *cucurbita moschata*; containing small amount of incomplete protein and large quantity of mineral elements, particularly potassium; having large alkali excess; rich in vitamin B.

Like all melon varieties the squash is a good food. Baked squash can be occasionally used to take the place of potatoes.

STRAWBERRIES

The wild variety, *fragaria vesca*, growing in prairies and woods is to be preferred because of their flavor and large mineral contents. However, there are many delicious varieties of strawberries, all of them rich in fruit sugar, minerals and alkaline elements. Strawberries contain potent bactericidal elements. Not even the deadly eberth typhus germ, when put into fresh strawberry juice, can exist more than a few hours. Some types of people, whose systems are unusually acid, suffer from a rash when eating strawberries. This is due to their over-sensitiveness to the protein in the strawberry. Besides being a delicious fruit dessert, strawberries have definite healing properties and can be highly recommended in all forms of gout and rheumatism. The French author, Fontenelle, who became one hundred years old, accredited his longevity to the liberal use of strawberries. The roots and leaves of the wild strawberry plant to this day are used in Central Europe. A brew of this kind takes the place of other teas and is recommended for intestinal difficulties.

SUGAR

All sugars belong to the carbohydrate family. Cane sugar, *saccharum officinarum*, came to us from India where, for hundreds of years, sugar has been used in its natural state. In 1747 Maggraf discovered the process of extracting sugar out of beets. Since then both the cane sugar and the beet sugar are used extensively in America. However, the unprocessed, unrefined, raw sugar, whether it is extracted from sugar cane or beets, is by far the most desirable to use because through the refining and bleaching process the alkaline bases of the sugar are lost.

White sugar is too concentrated and acid-forming a food. Children, especially, should be given the natural or raw sugar; uncooked honey or maple sugar make splendid sugar substitutes.

TEA

Thea sinensis comes to us from India, Ceylon, China and Japan. There are over twenty varieties, but here in America black tea and green tea are mostly used. Tea, like coffee, is a stimulant and when used occasionally is not harmful but excessive tea drinking discolors the skin and has a detrimental effect on the eyes. The Chinese people have an interesting way of preparing their tea. The tea leaves are covered with boiling water for exactly two minutes. This water is poured off and fresh water is added. In this manner most of the harmful tannin is eliminated.

TOMATOES

The fruit of *solanum lycopersicum* originated in its wild state in Peru. Since then many varieties have been cultivated and tomatoes have become one of our most important vegetables. They are rich in vitamines A, B and C; mineral salts and alkaline elements predominate. Tomatoes are best eaten raw and in salads, but canned tomatoes, especially the better brands, are to be preferred to the hot-house variety during the winter months. Because of the small amount of oxalic acid some uninformed people claim that

tomatoes cause rheumatism. This is absolutely
false as, in many of the large sanitariums in
Europe, tomato juice is given for the elimination of all forms of rheumatism. Tomato juice
is also a cleanser for the liver and those wishing to reduce can make a splendid reducing
cocktail by adding a bit of fresh lemon juice to
tomato juice.

TURNIPS

Turnips, when small or medium sized make
a splendid substitute for potatoes. The percentage of assimilable food material is small but
the mineral content is fair. Turnips are best
when baked. The juice should not be poured
off. Turnip greens make a splendid cooked
vegetable. They should be prepared in a few
minutes much the same as spinach. Young raw
turnips are delicious when grated and used for
salads.

VEGETABLE OYSTER

Root of the *tragoqogon porrifolins;* fairly rich
in protein and sugar; mineral element content
unknown; having an apparently moderately
large alkali excess; vitamin content unknown.

These vegetables were formerly widely cultivated and eaten as carrots are now.

VINEGAR

Wine vinegar or vinegar made from apple
cider was already used by the Romans. Such

vinegars are not harmful but the artificially prepared vinegars, so much in use, have a tendency
to slow up digestion. Here in America, where
lemons are so reasonable and to be had all year
round, it is far better to use lemon juice in place
of vinegar. Lemon juice is not only a splendid
fruit acid but has valuable minerals.

WALNUT

Fruit of the *juglans nigra;* rich in valuable
protein, fat and starches; rich in potassium, calcium and magnesium and phosphorus and sulphur acids; having acid excess and small
amount or vitamin B with traces of vitamin A.

WALNUT, ENGLISH

Fruit of the *juglans regia;* rich in valuable
protein, fat and starches; rich in potassium, magnesium, calcium and phosphorus and sulphur
acids; having fairly large acid excess and small
amount of vitamin B with traces of vitamin A.

English walnuts are an excellent, concentrated
food, which on account of their rich protein and
acid excess should be eaten in small quantities
and always in combination with fruits. Many
believe that walnuts are not fattening because
they have a purgative effect and so prevent corpulency by ending constipation. This is a mistake since walnuts are rich in fat and their
purgative properties do not interfere with the
assimilation of their fatty content.

YEAST

Although yeast is recommended as a protein-supplying food it has, nevertheless, become known that its protein is poor in quality and that when eaten in quantities it causes violent diarrhea. Yeast does help to correct acid conditions in the intestines, because it destroys acid bacteria.

Yeast extracts are offered to the public as a tonic under many different, commercial names. They are, however, entirely unnecessary in a well-balanced diet.

ALKALINE AND ACID FORMING FOODS

HERE, in America, most adults suffer from some form of acidosis. This is chiefly due to the fact that too many of the acid-forming foods are eaten. Statistics show that we eat about 70 per cent of such foods as meat, cheese, eggs, starches, and sugars, all of which are acid forming; and only consume about 30 per cent of the alkaline-forming foods, namely, fruits and vegetables.

A healthful diet should be exactly the reverse. We should consume about two-thirds of the alkaline-forming foods and only one-third of the acid-forming foods. Following these proportions the body will keep its alkaline predominance at all times, and excess acidity eliminates itself.

It seems a shame that American housewives, who have the best of foods at their disposal the year round, still insist upon throwing away the most valuable part of their foods. Vegetables are prepared in such a manner that the important alkaline elements are poured into the sink. A great many delicious foods are made unhealthful by adding great quantities of white sugar to them.

Milk, an alkaline food, becomes more or less neutral, or even acid forming when boiled too long or sterilized.

The housewife who wishes to have a healthy
family should remember to steam her vegetables
in their own juices for not more than 10 or 15
minutes, and never to pour off the juices in which
the vegetables have been cooked. And, she
should be sure that the menu for each meal includes some raw fruits or vegetables.

ACID-FORMING FOODS

Almonds (Unpeeled)

Anchovies

Artichokes

Asparagus Tips

Bacon

Beef, Fat

Beef, Lean

Beer

Biscuits

Bread, all kinds

Brussels Sprouts

Butter

Caviar

Cheese

Cheese, Cream

Cheese, Edam

Chicken

Chocolate

Cocoanuts

Corn

Cream

Eggs

Farina

Fish

Goose

Goose Grease

Goose-liver Paste

Grapenuts

Ham

Hazelnuts

Herring

Kellogg's Corn
   Flakes

Legumes

Lentils

Lobster

Macaroni

Margarine

Meat Extract

Oats

Oysters

Peanuts

Peas, Dried

Pigeons

Pork

Quaker Oats

Rice	Veal
Rye	Walnuts
Sardines	White Flour

Since the aforementioned foods are all acid-forming they should be overbalanced by the alkaline forming foods. Two-thirds of alkaline foods and one-third acid forming foods is a healthful combination.

ALKALINE-FORMING FOODS

Apple Cider
Apples
Apricots
Bananas (ripe)
Beans, Green
Beans, Soya
Beets, Red
Beet Sugar (unrefined)
Blackberries
Blood
Blueberries
Blueberry Wine
Buttermilk
Cabbage, Curly
Cabbage, Red
Cabbage, White
Carrots
Cauliflower
Celery
Cherries
Chestnuts, Baked
Chives
Coffee, Black
Cranberries
Cucumbers
Currants, Black
Currants, Dried
Currants, Red
Dandelion Greens
Dates
Endives
Figs, Dried

Gooseberries
Grapes
Head Lettuce
Honey, Pure
Horseradish
Kohlrabi
Leek
Lemons, Ripe
Malt Sugar
Melons
Milk, Cow's (Raw)
Milk, Goat's
Milk, Mother's
Milk, Skimmed
Mushrooms
Olives, Ripe
Onions
Oranges
Peaches
Pears
Peas, Fresh
Pineapple
Plums
Potatoes, Baked
Pumpkin
Radishes
Radishes, Black
Radishes, White
Raisins
Raspberries
Raspberry Juice
Rock Candy, Natural

Romaine	Tangerines
Salads, Green	Tomatoes
Sauerkraut	Turnips
Spinach	Watercress
Strawberries	Wine, Red
Sugar, Raw	Yoghurt

The above foods are our chief sources of the alkaline-forming elements. A diet that is made up of these foods constitutes an anti-toxic, or eliminative diet, which flushes the body of excess acidity.

THOSE ALL-IMPORTANT VITAMINS

VITAMINS have existed since the beginning of time, but we did not realize their tremendous importance until we began to eat foods that did not contain them. Man lost interest in foods when his inventive genius found an outlet and he discovered it was more profitable from a money-making standpoint to remove the life principle from many foods so that foodstuffs could be packed and shipped over a larger territory. The beginning of the mechanical age, in which we are now living, was the beginning of a decline in natural health. Just as soon as that life principle was destroyed and artificial foods became popular, all kinds of diseases that are the result of malnutrition sprang into existence. Physicians and food scientists went so deeply into the matter that they found out why we could not live without vitamins—what each living element in food did for us—and where every element could be found. To simplify their findings, the scientists listed the vitamin-containing foods in groups—each food group containing a particular vitamin throughout. The vitamin groups were differentiated by letters alphabetically arranged. Casimir Funk was the first scientist who experimented with the now well-known vitamins.

At the present time the best known vitamins are Vitamin "A," Vitamin "B," Vitamin "C," Vitamin "D" and Vitamin "E." Each one of these has a specific purpose to perform in the process of nutrition. Without these vitamins all the other foods we eat do not rebuild our bodies. Many thin people have gorged themselves with fattening foods, hoping to put on a few pounds. Fat people have gone from one diet to another hoping to reduce, and too many times the results for both types of diet have been disappointing. This was because of a lack of vitamins, without which other foods were unable to accomplish their tasks.

VITAMIN "A"

Vitamin "A" is an important one. It aids growth and is necessary for reproduction, so is vital to those wishing to stay young and healthy. Experiments have shown that individuals deprived of Vitamin "A" are easily affected with glandular troubles. Continued shortage of Vitamin "A" often causes a pus condition; also diseases of the liver, kidneys, ovaries, prostrate, testicles, lungs, etc.

Vitamin "A" has three vital tasks to perform. It helps to prolong life, it assists in rebuilding new cells, and it induces growth. Because of the last-named task, this vitamin is very necessary for children. The best Vitamin "A" foods are:

Tomatoes
Tomato Juice Cocktail
Raw Carrots
Carrot Juice Cocktail
Spinach (cooked not
  more than 8 minutes)

Certified Milk (from
  well-fed cows)
Butter
Fresh Egg Yolks
Cream
Cod Liver Oil

VITAMIN "B"

Vitamin "B" helps to revitalize the nervous system. Vitamin "B" has performed modern miracles in all sorts of nervous conditions. It aids in vitalizing the heart, liver, and kidneys, and helps to keep the all-important glands in youthful condition. We find an abundance of fine foods that are rich in Vitamin "B" which help to keep us fit.

The best Vitamin "B" foods are:

Fresh Spinach
Fresh Raw Cabbage
Fresh Raw Tomatoes
Tomato Juice Cocktail
Kidney Beans
Navy Beans
Raw Carrots
Raw Turnips

Fish Roe
Whole Rice
Whole Corn
Whole Bran
Calf's Liver
Sweetbreads
All Fresh Leafy Green
  Vegetables

Yeast Extracts

VITAMIN "C"

Everyone needs Vitamin "C" to keep the blood-stream in a healthy condition. Many are familiar with the dread disease called scurvy, which often attacks sailors, miners and all those who live on an unbalanced diet. Children are relieved of this terrible condition as soon as we supply Vitamin "C." It seems to energize and vitalize the entire body. Children who receive pasteurized milk must be given additional Vitamin "C" foods, as pasteurized milk does not supply Vitamin "C." Gum troubles, loose teeth and many other unhealthy conditions show a distinct lack of vitamin "C." We find this Vitamin especially in growing things. This is sure proof that vitamins are living processes which, when taken into the body, give us added energy. With the exception of cod liver oil and raw meat juice, Vitamin "C" is found chiefly in growing and sprouting vegetables.

The best Vitamin "C" foods are:

Lime Juice	Fresh String Beans
Lemon Juice	Raspberry Juice
Orange Juice	Oat Sprouts
Grapefruit Juice	Pea Sprouts
Watercress	Lentil Sprouts
Raw Cabbage	Bean Sprouts
Raw Tomatoes	Onions
Canned Tomatoes	Dandelions
Tomato Juice Cocktail	Endive

Raw Carrots

VITAMIN "D"

Vitamin "D" is particularly important for bone growth. Baby foods are too often devoid of this vitamin and as a result many children suffer from rickets. Pasteurized milk also lacks Vitamin "D," so other foods should be used to supply this deficiency if you do not use raw, or certified milk. Cod liver oil is rich in Vitamin "D" so if you cannot obtain the more tasty foods, rely on cod liver oil for your supply of vitamin "D." The life spark in Vitamin "D" also aids sufferers troubled with sleeplessness and restlessness. These people should be sure to eat plentifully of the foods containing this vitamin. The best Vitamin "D" foods are:

Butter	Cod Liver Oil
Cream	Salmon
Cocoanuts	Spinach
Cocoanut Oil	Swiss Chard
Tuna Fish	Dandelions
Cod Fish	Egg Yolk

and *An Abundance of Sunlight*

VITAMIN "E"

Last, but not least, is Vitamin "E," one of the newer discoveries in food science. This is a powerfully vitalizing vitamin, tremendously important in maintaining health and youthfulness. People who have used Vitamin "E" in large amounts report strength and energy. Animals given Vitamin "E" produce vital, healthy offspring. This new vitamin is found in the germ of wheat kernels when freshly ground.

The foods containing Vitamin "E" are:

Red Meats	Olive Oil
Green Leaves	Cotton Seed Oil
Butter Fat	Cocoanut Oil

Considering all of the foods in the vitamin groups given here, you notice that these essential sparks are found chiefly in fresh, growing, living foods. Some of the formerly despised green things are at last coming into their own, because they contain the precious elements that sustain life—mineral salts and those vital sparks —the vitamins.

You do not have to become a health crank to follow these principles. More and more people the world over are realizing that food can make or break us and that by eating abundantly of the living foods our bodies become vital and healthy.

HOW LONG THE DIFFERENT FOODS
REMAIN IN THE STOMACH

Strained Fruit Juices......................⎫
Potassium Broth...........................⎪
Plain Water...............................⎪
Black Coffee..............................⎬ 1 to 2 hours
Light Wine................................⎪
Raw Egg Yolk..............................⎪
Soft Boiled Egg...........................⎭

Eggs, Scrambled or Omelet.................⎫
Asparagus, Cauliflower, Boiled Potatoes ⎪
Stewed Cherries...........................⎬ 2 to 3 hours
Raw Oysters...............................⎪
Coffee with Cream, Boiled Milk............⎪
White Bread, Biscuits.....................⎭

Cucumbers, Radishes.......................⎫
Carrots, Turnips, Spinach.................⎪
Apples, Cherries..........................⎬ 3 to 4 hours
Rye Bread, Whole Wheat Bread..............⎪
Chicken, Squab, Rare Steak................⎭

Fried Chicken, Duck, Goose................⎫
Fried Steak, Smoked Fish and Meats,   ⎪
  Salty Fish..............................⎬ 4 to 5 hours
Bean or Pea Puree.........................⎪
Fried Rabbit..............................⎭

The above chart is very helpful to anyone
troubled with indigestion. Strained fruit juices,

potassium broth and raw egg yolk are, as you see, some of the more easily digested foods. Those with digestive troubles will do well to use the easily digested foods. Raw egg yolk and orange juice, and egg yolk beaten into potassium broth, are very nourishing and do not require much energy for digestion. Fried and salty meats are hardest to digest and should not be used by those having digestive troubles.

INDEX

133

See this full line of NATURAL HEALTH books at your dealer, or order direct from:

BENEDICT LUST PUBLICATIONS
P. O. Box 368
Beaumont, California 92223

BENEFICIAL BOOKS, series

Drink Your Troubles Away, John Lust	95¢
The Grape Cure, Johanna Brandt	95¢
Rational Fasting, Prof. Arnold Ehret	95¢
Mucusless Diet Healing System, Prof. Arnold Ehret	95¢
Make Your Juicer Your Drug Store, Dr. L. Newman	95¢
Dictionary of Foods, Ragnar Berg & Gaylord Hauser	95¢
Keener Vision Without Glasses, Gaylord Hauser	95¢

LUST PUBLICATIONS

The New Raw Juice Therapy, John B. Lust	3.00
Blood Washing Method, Dr. B. Lust	1.00
Kneipp Herbs, Dr. B. Lust	75¢
Internal Uncleanliness of Man, Prof. Arnold Ehret	2.00
Hope for the Arthritic, L. Lopez	1.00
Royal Jelly Miracle, Allen & Lust	1.00
Grandma's Kitchen Was Her Drugstore, Virginia Lust	1.00
About Scientific Fasting, Dr. L. Hazzard	1.00
Your Memory, Dr. B. Lust	75¢

Please add 25¢ when ordered by mail.